# Kites, Crackers and Craftsmen

☆Fifty Traditional Tokyo Shops
☆Maps with Regional Histories
☆Shopping Hints

by
Camy Condon
Kimiko Nagasawa

SHUFUNOTOMO CO., LTD.
Tokyo, Japan.

*Seventh printing, 1984*

*Published by Shufunotomo Co., Ltd.*
*1-chome, Surugada: Kanda, Chiyoda-ku,*
*Tokyo, 101 Japan*
*Printed in Japan*

*ISBN4-07-971732-6*

# Shopping for History

After arriving in Tokyo in 1969, I explored my new neighborhood for some of the Made-in-Japan bargains so familiar in the U.S.: stainless steel utensils, brass lamps, wind chimes, paper lanterns, pottery coffee mugs, etc. It took only three such outings to discover that this imported image of what to expect in a Tokyo shop was all wrong and that the great majority of Japanese items sold in the U.S. are made for export only. They are not representative of the things in Tokyo shops, nor are they of particular interest to the modern Japanese housewife who prefers oven-proof "western" style casseroles to locally made pottery.

After an initial period of mild disappointment and introspective questioning ("What is Japanese?"), assuaged by a few tourist purchases from hotel arcades and 2 stores catering to like-minded, misguided foreigners (those places *did* sell summer fans all year round), I reluctantly set aside my image of what ought to be sold, and began to appreciate what is here. I started with an essential—food—and that interest plus the good fortune of living near Kimiko Nagasawa led to our collaboration in the writing of *Eating Cheap in Japan*.

Our publishers encouraged us to write another book—this time a photographic shopping guide. We agreed, eager to write about shops that were very traditional and uniquely Japanese; we wanted to include only family businesses which had been handed down from father to son for several generations. Searching for the unique and traditional in Tokyo often led us into paradox. One day I would uncover a rare find, and the next day we would learn about seven similar shops just down the street. Then Nagasawa-san would hear of what seemed to be an ideal choice—a business 6 generations old, still in the family, making and selling a single product; we would visit "the little shop" and find a 6-story glass and steel building . . . not quite what we had in mind.

*Kites, Crackers and Craftsmen* turned out to be as varied a collection as . . . well, 50 family shops anywhere. The

1

shops we have chosen are typical of others all over Japan for their perseverance and their emphasis on family over profitmaking. A few are among the last of their kind. Ask the kite-maker or the carver of wooden combs, and they will name, counting on the fingers of one hand, all the others in Japan. Most of these shops are well known in their neighborhoods, and a few are nationally famous. All of the shops have in common the making and selling of items which are uniquely Japanese.

In the limited space of this small book we have tried to describe a little of the family history and hint at the extraordinary skill and effort that characterizes the workmanship in each business. We hope to intrigue you, to encourage you to visit these shops or others like them. Knowing a little about the making of rice crackers, wooden clogs, *tatami* mats, combs, kimono and *obi* and folkcraft, will lead you into the cultural heart of Japan. Window shopping in this way can truly be a lesson in Japanese history. For the foreigner, these shops provide one of the few easily accessible contacts with traditional aspects of Tokyo life so often obscured by a façade of modern "western" imitation.

Camy Condon
Tokyo, 1973

The Japanese style of writing names is to place the family name before the given name. In this book we have followed the Japanese style for important historical figures like Tokugawa Ieyasu; all other names are written in western style.

# Dedication

To Atsuko, Christina, Michael and Nobuhiro with love from your mothers. We hope that when you grow up these shops will still be here to welcome you.

# Acknowledgements

The authors wish to acknowledge the assistance of the many persons who aided in the preparation of this book. We are particularly grateful to Mr. Mikio Sasaki for his excellent photographs, to our talented editor Miss Kikue Narita, and to the entire staff of the Shufunotomo International Department whose competence in several languages and interest in international readership make possible the publication of books of this kind. We wish to acknowledge three standard sources of background information: Mock Joya's *Things Japanese* (Tokyo News Service), Kenkichi Kusumoto's *Nippon no Ichiryuhin* (Perikan-sha) and Edwin O. Reischauer's *Japan Past and Present* (Charles E. Tuttle Co.). In addition we were helped by the kind advice of Mr. and Mrs. Jiro Aoyama and Mrs. Shotaro Uchiyama, and the cooperation of Mrs. Laura Oberdorfer who did the final English editing. Finally we wish to recognize the generosity of the many Tokyo shop owners who told us their fascinating family histories, some of which could not be included due to lack of space.

# Table of Contents

## Nihonbashi Area

**Benmatsu** (box lunches), **Fujiwara Obiji-ten** (Japanese women's sashes), **Haibara** (stationery, hand-made paper), **Kammo** (fish paste products), **Misucho** (bamboo shades), **Token Shibata** (swords and armor), **Tsuikawa Gakkiten** (Japanese harp), **Yagicho** (dried bonito fish).

## Ginza-Tsukiji Area

**Itoh Oke-ten** (wooden tubs and buckets), **Kashiwa-ya** (paper lanterns), **Kuno-ya** (kimono accessories), **Kyu-kyo-do** (incense), **Masuda-ya** (kimono, *haori* and *obi* cloth), **Ohno-ya Sohon-ten** (traditional socks), **Ryuzen-do** (tea ceremony utensils), **Tsumugi-ya** (hand spun silk).

## Other Areas

**Bingo-ya** (folkcrafts), **Aoki Uemon Shoten** (straw mats), **Maezawa Goban-ten** (*go* boards and stones), **Ishida Biwa-ten** (Japanese lute), **Nagasawa In-ten** (family and business seals).

## Appendix

Nearly every visitor to Tokyo knows the site—the enormous red paper lantern, the two fearsome guardian gods, and the pair of giant straw sandals that mark the gateway to the 1,300-year-old Asakusa Kannon temple. From this gate there stretches the famous Nakamise Street, lined with colorful shops and stands selling souvenirs, toys, handbags, clothing and food. The atmosphere is festive, the feeling is of old Edo. Most of the shops here sell items that are not very different from those found throughout Japan. But here and there along Nakamise Street and elsewhere in Asakusa are shops with long and fascinating histories, shops whose proud owners continue to make traditional objects by hand. We can mention only a few, all of which can be visited on a leisurely afternoon stroll.

Asakusa (pronounced *ah-sock'-sah*) is famous, not just for such shops, but even more as one of Tokyo's major (and cheaper) amusement centers. It was here that in 1933 the first movie was shown in Japan. Today Asakusa is famous for its many movie and vaudeville theaters. Its countless bars, cabarets and lovers' hotels are remnants of the Yoshiwara, the famous red-light district that was outlawed just after World War II.

At the edges of Asakusa are other historical sites. To the south is the Kokugi-kan where *sumo* tournaments are held. To the east is the once idyllic, but now polluted, Sumida River. And to the west is Ueno Park, where the Tokugawa volunteer army was defeated by the powerful Meiji forces.

By subway Asakusa is only a few minutes away from the glass and steel structures of modern Tokyo, but the mood of Asakusa is years away!

6

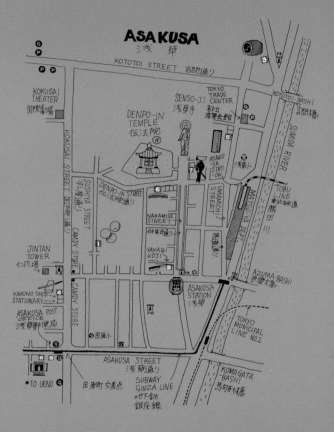

# Iriyama Sembei

13-4 Asakusa 1-chome Taito-ku.      Tel 844-1376.
**Hours:** 10: 00–6: 00 (Closed Thur.).      Founded 1917.
**Specialty:** rice crackers (*sembei*).
Owner: Tatsundo Yamazaki (plus mother, younger brother, wife and 8 employees).

For more than 400 years the crunchy rice cracker has been an essential part of Japanese daily life. It is often munched over a friendly cup of hot green tea and is enjoyed at any hour of the day or night by both children and adults. Made of high gluten rice and soy sauce, over fifteen varieties are sold throughout Japan. At IRIYAMA SEMBEI you will find only one kind, a cracker with an uneven shape and an unusually hard, crispy texture. It is roasted over high heat produced by special charcoal called *bincho* from Wakayama Prefecture. Come between 10: 00 am–1: 00 pm or 3: 00 pm–6: 00 pm, and you will see several members of the Yamazaki family bending over the charcoal braziers, skillfully turning over the golden crackers.

A generation ago the shop's founder, the son of a wealthy family in the landed class, abandoned his university studies to become a merchant. Buying a small *sembei* business belonging to an elderly couple, he experimented with different ways of roasting the crackers and finally developed the special method used today.

**Shopping Hints:**                    **Price range: ¥40 each**

—The best *sembei* are a glowing amber shade called *kitsune-iro*, the color of a fox.
—To allow the moisture to escape, *sembei* are wrapped while still warm in plain paper. After one hour of cooling they should be put into the plastic bag provided; this preserves the crispiness for as long as one month.
—You may purchase one cracker, *ichi-mai*, or standard quantities of 5 for ¥200, or 30 in a special gift canister costing ¥1,400.
—The busiest season of the year is from December 1 to 25, the time of the obligatory year-end exchange of gifts, *O-seibo*.

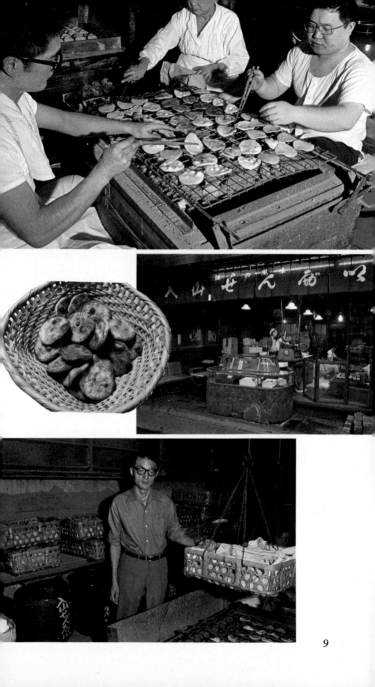

# Kaneso

18-12 Asakusa 1-chome Taito-ku.     Tel. 844-1379.
**Hours:** 10:00–8:30 (Closed Thur.).     Founded 1853.
**Specialty:** cutlery (*hocho*).
Owner: Eizo Hirano (plus nephew and 6 craftsmen).

Long ago in Kansai, Jingoro Hirano learned a special method of tempering metals. He brought his skill to Tokyo and opened a cutlery shop which his great grandson runs today. KANESO, a tiny V-shaped shop, carries over 100 kinds of knives, including the 20 most commonly used for cooking. (Until recent times the Japanese housewife required 5 knives to prepare the food used in the daily meals, but today she often gets by with 1 or 2.)

The traditional Japanese knife is made from steel and crude iron heated together over extremely high heat. KANESO prides itself on using the *hon-yaki* method of tempering the blade, the same technique used in making fine swords. During the tempering process the metal is encased in a special mud-pack to protect it from overheating and breaking.     Western knives, also sold at KANESO, are made only of steel heated at a moderate temperature.

Kicho Shimane, a noted authority on the artistic cutting of vegetables, once carved a large goldfish from a giant radish and presented it to the shop. Placed in a tank with water and seaweed, the fish was so life-like that a customer observed, "This must indeed be a very splendid fish! It swims as gently and quietly as a kingly man."

**Shopping Hints:**          **Price range: ¥1,000– ¥500,000**
—In testing fine cutlery one should examine the hardness, flexibility and strength of the blade.
—Ask for an *unagi saki* to cut an eel, a *hugu hiki* to cut a blowfish and *sashimi bocho* to slice fresh raw fish.
—If you are in the market for something large, ask to see the 2½-foot butcher knife, *niku-kiri-bocho*, used chiefly for display purposes in butcher shops.
—Cutting tools for craftsmen (shoemakers, etc.) are also available.

# Miyamoto Unosuke Shoten Map (p. 7, Asakusa #3)

1-15 Asakusa 6-chome Taito-ku.          Tel. 874-4131.
**Hours:** 8: 10–5: 10 (Closed Sun. and Hols.).     Founded 1843.
**Specialty:** festival drums and portable shrines (*taiko* and
    *mikoshi*).
Owner: Kenji Miyamoto (plus wife, son and 25 employees).

Many important religious sites use this large and im-
pressive shop's shrines and drums. Meiji Shrine and the
Imperial Court are two of its best customers, and the
1964 Olympics were opened with *gagaku* drums made here.

There are two categories of Japanese drums: *ohdaiko*,
usually large, barrel-shaped drums with cowhide tacked to
each end; and *itojime-daiko*, smaller, hourglass-shaped
drums which have horsehide coverings strung together with
a silk cord. *Ohdaiko* are used in both Shinto and Buddhist
ceremonies. Although the drum itself is rather plain, its
wooden stand is often carved and decorated. The most
popular kind of *itojime-daiko* is the *tsuzumi* used in *noh*
and *kabuki* dramas. It is held over the shoulder and
played with one hand.

*Mikoshi*, the portable tabernacle-like shrines jostled
around at festivals (by a required 60 people or more), are
ordered in the spring for formal dedication in the fall.
*Jibori*-style is decorated with engraved bronze or copper,
while *uchimono*-style uses cheaper molded sheets of metal.
About 200 *mikoshi*, whose minimum cost is ¥300,000, are
sold by the Miyamoto family each year.

**Shopping Hints:**          **Price range: up to ¥10,000,000**
—The shop also sells papier-mache masks. The fat-cheeked
  woman is *okame*, the round-eyed man with the off-center
  mouth is *hyottoko* and the demon is an *oni*. These masks
  are used in *kagura*, an old form of humorous entertainment
  performed at shrines on certain festival days. Each costs
  ¥1,200.
—Ornamental bells and a festival lion costume, meant to cover
  a string of dancing children, can also be purchased.
—For the appropriate accompaniment to a rice-planting
  ceremony you should purchase a *dengaku-daiko*.

12

# Toishi-ya

8-14 Nishi Asakusa 1-chome Taito-ku.     Tel. 841-1014.
**Hours:** 9: 00–7: 30 (Open every day).     Founded 1573.
**Specialty:** whetstones (*toishi*).
Owner: Hiroshi Nomura (plus 4 employees).

The many stone slabs and the grinding wheels that fill
the little shop seem prosaic enough, but the shop itself has
a romantic history. TOISHI-YA was established four
hundred years ago at a Kyoto crossroads to serve *samurai*
in search of a place to sharpen their swords. The motto,
THIS IS THE PLACE TO SHARPEN YOUR SPIRIT, was carved on
a wooden plaque that can be seen today in the back of
the shop. To the *samurai*, the spirit and the sword were
indeed symbolic equivalents.

TOISHI-YA moved to Tokyo when it became the
capital. The shop has served sculptors, carvers, craftsmen,
chefs and workers in the Asakusa area for more than 100
years. Four generations have maintained the tradition of
locating and cutting out fine whetstones from a small area
in Kyoto Prefecture where the river beds produce a finely
grained and layered slate and sandstone. One whetstone
owned by the shop is valued at ¥8,000,000, and another
was awarded first prize in a German competition.

Nomura-san recalls an evening with Miyairi Shohei, a
famous swordsmith, who often came to sharpen his old
and precious sword on the best stone in the shop. That
night he darkened the room and held the whetted sword
up to the light of the full moon which came flooding in
through the window. The sword glistened in the moonlight
and reflected a "brilliant blue flash." "I can remember the
scene as though it were today," reports the owner.

**Shopping Hints:**          **Price range: ¥150–¥8,000,000**
—There are three grades of whetstones: rough (blue or black),
  medium (blue or grayish white), and fine (usually yellow).
—For general use, the medium-grade stone is best. Ask for a
  *naka-to*, a bargain at ¥350. (The same stone costs twice as
  much in department stores.)

# Yamamoto Soroban-ten Map (p. 7, Asakusa #5)

2-35 Asakusa Taito-ku.    Tel. 841-7503.
**Hours:** 9: 30–6: 00 (Closed Sun.).    Founded 1913.
**Specialty:** Japanese abacuses (*soroban*).
Owner: Kinjiro Kudo (plus wife, daughter and 3 employees).

A number of years ago a new calculating machine was pitted against the Japanese abacus, and the abacus won. Today, this little portable calculator is still an essential item in banks, department stores, restaurants and bars in Japan. Its use is taught in every school, often beginning in the 7th grade, and a high-grade certificate of abacus competence is required for some of the better financial jobs.

An eye-catching 4-foot abacus in the window and a giant 7-foot abacus by the front door mark the site of YAMAMOTO SOROBAN-TEN. Mrs. Kudo opened the shop 60 years ago as a family stationery store to help supplement the monthly income. Then Mr. Kudo started making abacuses as a hobby. Gradually other supplies were eliminated, and the shop began to deal exclusively in *soroban*. Mr. Kudo no longer makes *soroban* himself. Most of the ones in his shop today are made by farm families from the mountainous regions of Shimane and Hyogo Prefectures. The Kudo family has on display a few unusual *soroban*, including one used by the blind.

**Shopping Hints:**                **Price range: ¥200–¥100,000**
—There are three major types of abacuses: one for the office, one for the shop and a pocket-size one.
—A good abacus is determined by the correct fitting of the movable beads on the bamboo spindles.
—Boxwood and birch are the most popular woods used in making abacuses. If you want something more expensive, ask for one made of red sandalwood or ebony; and if you have ¥100,000 to spend, you may order one in ivory.
—*Unshu soroban* from Shimane Prefecture are better than *banshu soroban* from Hyogo.
—Located across the street from YONO-YA, the branch store is housed in a charming old building worth glancing at.

# Yono-ya

37-10 Asakusa 1-chome Taito-ku.    Tel. 844-1755.
**Hours:** 9:00–8:00 (Open every day).    Founded 1673.
**Specialty:** traditional combs (*kushi*).
Owner: Mitsumasa Minekawa (plus father, wife and 2 crafts-men, both over 70 years of age).

The time-worn exterior of YONO-YA and the soft yellow glow of the combs displayed within give dignity to a shop which is one of the few vestiges of early Tokyo in the area. YONO-YA moved from Saitama Prefecture to Edo in 1690 and has been at its present location for 80 years. During its long history many famous *kabuki* and *shimpa* actors have entered its doors; today's customers are usually housewives who cling to old ways of caring for their hair and value a hand-made comb. There are only three other traditional comb shops in all Japan, one near Ueno Station in Tokyo and the other two in Kyoto.

Originally a mark of sacredness and later a symbol of a woman's married status, combs were introduced to Japan from China and became popular during the Tokugawa Period. For many years the comb was seen as a charm to protect the honor and virtue of its wearer. Lingering on today is the belief that it is bad luck to pick up a lost comb or to give a comb as a gift.

YONO-YA sells more than 200 kinds of combs. *Toki-gushi* are used for arranging the hair; *sashi-gushi* are decorative combs. There are two styles of *sashi-gushi*: a long hairpin-like comb, and a round half-moon shape. Crests usually decorate *sashi-gushi*. In the past you used a family crest, but today you may select any you like.

**Shopping Hints:**    Price range: ¥680–¥6,000
—Combs made of *tsuge* (boxwood) are a lighter color and are more expensive than those made of *tsubaki* (camellia). (The wood is thoroughly dried before the combs are made—sometimes for as long as 30 years.)
—A really good comb should never be washed. Clean it by wiping carefully with a soft cloth.
—A general purpose comb is called *tokigushi no sashiara*.

19

# Sukeroku

Map (p. 7, Asakusa #7)

3-1 Asakusa 2-chome Taito-ku.　　Tel. 844-0542.
**Hours:** 12 : 00–6 : 00 (Closed Fri.).　　Founded 1773.
**Specialty:** hand-made miniatures of Edo Period life (*Edo-shumi kogangu*).
Owner: Tamae Kimura (plus husband, son and 20 craftsmen).

In this splendid little shop are marvelously detailed hand-made miniatures of street peddlers, kite shops, restaurants, candy stands, tiny dolls, festival ornaments, wigs, combs, folk toys and animals. Each tells a little story of daily life in Tokyo 100 years ago.

SUKEROKU was originally a used bookshop whose founder sold dolls at night stalls as a side-line. These Edo-style dolls, larger than those made today, became popular with *samurai* families. When members of the rising merchant class began to imitate the life-style of the *samurai*, the Tokugawa government clamped restrictions on their display of wealth. The merchants, however, devised clever ways of hiding their riches: they lined cheap kimono with expensive silk, they placed elaborate ornamentation on the insides of letter boxes—and they reduced the size of the popular dolls so that they could be hidden conveniently.

Before the war there were a number of other shops that made Edo-style folkcraft, but most were destroyed by bombs. Kimura-san, now 78, recalls his thoughts as he viewed the ruins of Asakusa: "I must begin again. There will be no one else to continue the tradition of miniature-making. Years ago there were many people to consult about Edo life. They provided many helpful suggestions concerning the details of my miniatures, but now these people are dead. There is no one left who remembers."

Kimura-san is the only one who still makes *Edo no Tebineri*, wonderfully detailed clay figures of people and animals.

**Shopping Hints:**　　　　**Price range: ¥200–¥500,000**
—You may select from more than 1,000 kinds of miniatures.
—The most expensive item, a set of Girls' Day Dolls made of wood, costs ¥35,000.

20

# Hamada Shoten

10-9 Kotobuki 2-chome Taito-ku. Tel 841-4965.
**Hours:** 8: 30–6: 00 (Closed 10th and 25th.). Founded 1873.
**Specialty:** Buddhist family altars and Shinto shrines (*butsugu*).
Owner: Hiroshi Yoshiaki (plus 12 salesmen and 17 craftsmen).

HAMADA-SHOTEN has two workshops, one producing the Buddhist family altars called *butsudan* and the other making Shinto shrines. To avoid bad luck and rivalry among the deities, the Shinto shrines are sold in a second shop a few doors away from the *butsudan* shop.

*Butsudan* are made of various woods including mulberry, cherry and sandalwood; inexpensive plastic altars are made to look like these woods. Tokyo-style *butsudan* are rather plain with the dark wood polished to reveal the grain; while Kyoto-style altars, which can be very large, have a lacquer finish and gold-leaf interior. Each of the many sects within Buddhism has its own cabinet altars with somewhat different accessories inside. In general, you will find a scroll or statue of Buddha, Kannon, Nichiren or Amida; tablets with the names of deceased family members; a miniature offering table; a tiny cup for water or tea; a little rice bowl; a gong; a flower vase, incense stand and box.

You should purchase your *butsudan* on an auspicious occasion, preferably at the spring or fall equinox or during the summer *o-bon* season.

**Shopping Hints:** **Price range: ¥2,000–¥10,000,000**
—Plastic altars start at ¥15,000. Tokyo-style wood *butsudan* cost from ¥20,000 to ¥5,000,000. Lacquered Kyoto-style *butsudan* are ¥500,000 to ¥10,000,000.
—Lacquered wood tablets for the names of the dead cost ¥1,500 to ¥50,000. Plastic prayer beads are ¥100 and up; crystal ones start at ¥3,000; amber beads are ¥100,000 or more. The doll-like offering dishes, called *reiku-zen*, may be purchased for as little as ¥1,500.
—Shinto shrines, copies of Kotai Jingu at Ise, cost between ¥4,000 and ¥1,000,000. Shrines for the fire god, Kojin-sama, begin at ¥2,000.

# UENO

"Ueno" means upper field or heights. The area became an important Edo district after the Tokugawa family built the Kan-eiji Temple to protect Edo Castle from demon-inspired calamities approaching from the northeast. (The northeast direction is called *kimon*, or devil's gate, and even today it is thought to bring evil to families—particularly to the eldest son. The southwest direction is disastrous for the mistress.) For many years the wide street going out from Kan-eiji Temple was the major route for all imperial and noble processions going to and coming from the castle. By the end of the 17th century this street was one of the busiest in Edo, lined with shops of every kind and filled with peddlers, travelers and new residents.

Ueno was the site of the last battle of the civil war preceding the Meiji Restoration. Many young *samurai* defenders of the Tokugawa family lost their lives on its hills in a vain attempt to protect Edo Castle and Kan-eiji Temple, the last of the feudal holdings.

After the Meiji Restoration, Ueno was chosen as the location of Tokyo's first public park. Many cherry trees were planted, and each spring great crowds of the common people came to enjoy the blossoms. With the construction of the National Museum, Tokyo University of Art and Music, public halls, a zoo and other museums and galleries, the park has become a cultural center.

At the south end of Ueno Park is Shinobazu Pond. Once a swamp, it is today filled with a mat of water lilies. The district on two sides of the pond, called Ikenohata, was famous as a residential area for geisha. A few of the shops catering to geisha and their clients are still there today.

24

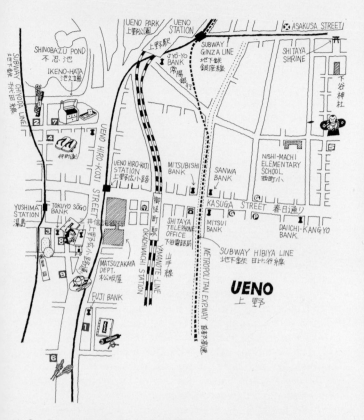

3. Enomoto-en 榎 本 園（徳陽相互銀行隣）
　　⇨pp. 30 & 31.
4. Hasegawa 長 谷 川（仲町通りを入り四つ角を左折）
　　⇨pp. 32 & 33.
5. Hashimoto 橋 本（御徒町駅より春日通り第一勧業銀行
　　斜め向い側を左に入る）⇨pp. 34 & 35.
6. Itoh Soh-hon-po 伊藤総本舗（文行堂の斜め向い）
　　⇨pp. 36 & 37.
7. Kyo-ya 京 屋（仲町通り）⇨pp. 38 & 39.
8. Sairaku-do 西 楽 堂（三井信託銀行裏）⇨pp. 40 & 41.
9. Usagi-ya うさぎ屋（広小路通り）⇨pp. 42 & 43.

# Bunkoh-do

16-4 Ueno 3-chome Taito-ku.     Tel 831-4661.
**Hours:** 10: 00–7: 00 (Closed Sun.).     Founded 1878.
**Specialty:** old books (*kosho*)
Owner: Bunjiro Yokoo (plus son).

Two or three fine old card-paintings in the window of this small shop entice even the foreigner who cannot read Japanese to enter and browse through the traditionally printed and bound books, hanging scrolls, card-paintings and old woodblock prints lovingly collected by BUNKOH-DO's owner.

Card-paintings are called *shikishi* if square-shaped and *tanzaku* if long and narrow. Collections of *tanzaku* bound into albums are called *tekagami*. *Tekagami* albums containing the writings of famous persons are often used to study calligraphic styles and can be extraordinarily valuable. The oldest *tekagami* at BUNKOH-DO dates back to the 10th century.

*Kosho*, or old books, are all of hand-made paper; the text is written or printed from wood blocks carved by hand. The pages are folded and bound to a simple front and back cover, or to a more elaborate 3-page cloth cover with a tiny clasp. The oldest book at BUNKOH-DO was handwritten at the end of the 16th century.

The scrolls at BUNKOH-DO are generally antique works by Buddhist priests or tea ceremony masters. *Tatemono* is the name for scrolls with long centers; *yokomono* scrolls have wide centers.

Old books and papers are obtained from rural areas where papers were kept safely during the war. They are bought and sold by Tokyo dealers in Kanda at the *Kosho-kai-kan* once a month.

**Shopping Hints:**         **Price range: ¥300–¥10,000,000**
—Old books cost from ¥500 to ¥100,000. *Tekagami* collections can be as expensive as ¥10,000,000.
—The long *tanzaku* cards are from ¥300 to ¥300,000. Square *shikishi* cards, woodblock prints and card paintings of *kabuki* actors begin at ¥1,000.

# Domyo

11-1 Ueno 2-chome Taito-ku.      Tel. 831-3773.
**Hours:** 10:00–5:00 (Open every day).      Founded 1652.
**Specialty:** decorative silk cords (*o-himo*).
Owner: **Issei** Yamaoka (plus 25 craftsmen for research in
·      Tokyo, and 350 craftsmen in Gumma Prefecture).

In 1652 Shimbei Echigoya, a descendant of *samurai*, moved from Niigata Prefecture to Edo and opened a shop selling cords for use on armor, helmets and swords. The demand for military gear was high, and for many years the shop prospered. However, with the passing of the Sword Abolition Law after the Meiji Restoration the need for military cords declined abruptly. Undaunted, DOMYO turned to making decorative cords for women. Traditional weaving methods and patterns were used, and the shop became known for its authentic patterns. In the late 1950's the Imperial Household Agency asked DOMYO to study ancient silk cords preserved in temples and the Imperial Repository in Nara. DOMYO craftsmen learned to reproduce exactly the ancient patterns, and in 1960 their ability was designated an Intangible National Property.

A single cord may require one month's work from four people. The simplest cord uses 4 spools with 24 threads in each strand of the braid. The most expensive cord uses 97 spools; 8 people produce only 3 cm. (about 1 inch) of this cord a day.

The Japanese art of weaving cords is incredibly ancient. Its history can be traced back as far as 7000 B.C. when braided strands were pressed into early Jomon pottery.

**Shopping Hints:**            **Price range: ¥1,300–¥300,000**
—*Obijime* cords, available in more than 420 ancient patterns, cost from **¥4,800** to ¥300,000.
—*Haori-jime*, the short cord that fastens the kimono jacket called *haori*, costs from **¥1,300 to ¥4,000.**
—*Sageo* are the decorative cords used on swords. They are woven to order in your choice of patterns and colors. Silk cords for hanging scrolls or for use as hinges on antique standing screens may also be ordered.

# Enomoto-en

Map (p. 25, Ueno #3)

17-7 Ueno 1-chome Taito-ku.     Tel. 831-8246.
**Hours:** 8:00–7:00 (Closed Sun.).     Founded 1873.
**Specialty:** green tea and rice crackers (*o-cha* and *o-sembei*).
Owner: Hirohito Enomoto (plus father, mother and wife).

Four generations ago Enomoto-san abandoned his thankless job as tax collector for the Takato clan and opened a shop selling green tea. The present owner, proud of his family's tradition of selling exclusively the fine green tea from Shizuoka Prefecture, gives particular attention to the good scent of the leaves when making his selection.

Just after World War II the Enomoto family began to sell home-made rice crackers, *o-sembei*, in a twin store next to the tea-shop. Once a week, starting at 5 a.m., the rice is ground, steamed, flattened and cut into various shapes. The cut dough is sun-dried on the roof for several hours (in winter there is an additional 1-week drying period indoors), and then it is toasted over charcoal.

**Shopping Hints:**
   **Price range: tea (¥100–¥1,000), crackers (¥20 for 3–¥22)**
—Tea is sold by the 100 grams (3½ oz.). *Gyokuro* is the best and most expensive; brew 1 minute in water 60°–70°C. *Sencha*, a medium-priced tea, is usually served to guests; brew 1 minute in 80°C. water. *Bancha* is for everyday use; brew 1 or more minutes in 100°C. water. *Hojicha* is roasted *bancha* with a brownish color and smoky flavor; brew as for *bancha*. *Gemmaicha* is *bancha* mixed with roasted, popped rice (looks like tiny popcorn—delicious); brew 1 minute in 90°C. water.
—*Kyusu*, teapots with a straight handle attached on one side, are also sold. The red *tokoname-yaki* are from Aichi Prefecture and the brown *banko-yaki* are from Mie Prefecture.
—Tea canisters with attractive designs painted on orange or black backgrounds are available from ¥180 to ¥450.
—There are 2 kinds of home-made crackers which you can buy individually or in a gift box. *Rokka-sen* are *sembei* cut into 6 traditional shapes (¥20 for 3 each). *Togarashi* are flavored with red pepper and sesame seeds (¥10 each). ENOMOTO-EN also sells many varieties of factory-made *sembei*.

# Hasegawa

4-4 Ueno 2-chome Taito-ku.     Tel. 831-3933.
**Hours:** 7:00–9:00 (Open every day).     Founded 1928.
**Specialty:** wooden clogs (*geta*).
Owner: Yosuke Mizutani (plus father).

HASEGAWA is one of 3 affiliated shops in Tokyo with the same name. The father of the present owner began to peddle *geta* in the streets of Ueno just after the great earthquake of 1923. Geisha who lived in the district were his good customers, for fashions in thongs changed rapidly and the geisha often asked him to renew theirs. The shop flourished till the 1950's when paved roads and western dress caused *geta* to decline in popularity. (Before that time wooden *geta* were worn by almost everyone, due to a Buddhist tradition prohibiting the use of leather.)

Lightweight *kiri* (paulownia) is the best wood for *geta*. The grain of the wood should run in parallel lines the length of the *geta*. A medium-priced clog may have 12 to 16 lines of grain, while the most expensive sometimes has more than 30. A single piece of wood is split in half to make a pair; the slightly curved flow of the grain is the only way to determine which clog is for the right foot and which is for the left, for otherwise the two are exactly the same. You may choose black-lacquered *geta*, but the best finish is a natural polish which shows off the grain.

**Shopping Hints:**     **Price range: ¥2,000–¥25,000**

—Ladies' *geta* include: *koma-geta*, the most common, ¥2,000–¥10,000; *komachi*, for girls from 17 to 20 years, ¥2,800; *ashida*, for rainy days, with plastic covers for the toes; *hiyori*, rather high, good for rainy days; *yuki-geta*, for snowy days, distinguished by the sharp angle of the 2 bars. Men's *geta*, wider than ladies', are called *kaku*. Priests wear *maru*, oval-shaped with rounded heels and toes. The thongs (*hanao*) for men and women are of silk or velvet; plastic and leather are also used for women.

—Paper umbrellas with bamboo ribs (*kasa*) are also sold at *geta* stores. HASEGAWA's are from Gifu Prefecture. *Bangasa* have golden-brown oiled paper (**¥2,000),** and *janome* have brightly colored oiled paper or silk (**¥5,000–¥10,000).**

# Hashimoto

25-6 Higashi Ueno 2-chome Taito-ku.     Tel. 831-2624.
**Hours:** 8:00–7:00 (Closed Sun.).     Founded 1890.
**Specialty:** kites (*tako*).
Owner: Teizo Hashimoto (plus wife).

The entry way of HASHIMOTO is cluttered with cartons of supplies. Hanging from the bamboo rafters of the small *tatami* room are brilliantly colored kites drying above the kerosene stove. And in the middle, surrounded by pots of paint, cans of brushes and three cats, is Hashimoto-san, a friendly, bespectacled man who learned to make kites from his father. As a young boy he particularly enjoyed sneaking out to fly one of the better kites, hiding it carefully under his kimono jacket to avoid a scolding.

The paintings on Hashimoto-san's kites are often inspired by *ukiyo-e* or *kabuki* figures and by his father's old designs. The most difficult part of kite making is to draw the outline of the painting on the handmade *washi* paper, and with a large kite this step may take an entire day. Next the colors are filled in—first yellow, then other light colors and finally the vivid reds. Then the bamboo frame is fitted onto the back, and 14 strings are sewn into place, tied and wound decoratively together.

In Tokyo, an association of kite lovers, called *Nippon-Tako-no-Kai*, sponsors kite-flying contests on the banks of the Tama River on New Year's Day, on Children's Day (May 5) and on Health-Sports Day (October 10).

**Shopping Hints:**                    **Price range:** ¥300–¥20,000
—Hand-painted kites begin at about ¥800. A large one without frame or strings, appropriate for framing, is ¥7,000. *Yakko-dako*, a cross-shaped kite painted as a bird or man, costs ¥800 to ¥1,500. You may order sets of 10 kites, each complete for flying or display and in its own box, for ¥10,000.
—Smaller kites with the outline of the design printed on the paper but painted in by hand are very inexpensive. A white kite with a huge red character meaning "dragon" is only ¥300.

# Itoh Sohonpo

Map (p. 25, Ueno #6)

16-7 Soto-kanda 6-chome Chiyoda-ku.     Tel. 831-4840.
**Hours:** 9 : 00–7 : 00 (Open every day).     Founded 1773.
**Specialty:** natural medicines made from charred animals and
plants (*kuroyaki*). Owner: Yoshiya Itoh (plus wife and daughter).

Large handwritten posters are stuck to the windows of
this corner house. An enormous turtle shell hangs by a
doorway, and inside you can see charred crocks and rows
of apothecary jars. This is a *kuroyaki-ya*, a shop selling
medicines made from charred plants and animals.

About 200 years ago, Japanese doctors began to study
the Chinese use of charred medicines. The Chinese
theorized that there are two aspects of the human body,
one positive and one negative, and that disease occurs
when there is an imbalance between the two. Certain
animals and plants that have been carbonized by burning
acquire the power to cure such disease. The Japanese
version of this theory and practice, called *kokan-igaku*, was
popular in the 19th century. Thought by many to be only a
folk belief, *kokan-igaku* brings relief to others who have
not been helped by modern western medicines.

ITOH-SOHONPO produces more than 400 kinds of
natural remedies. Animals, insects and reptiles are the
most important ingredients. Bark, roots and herbs are also
used. These substances are placed in earthenware pots,
covered with rice straw and set into holes in the ground.
The straw is burned slowly for many hours. The essence
thus produced is taken medicinally in powdered form.

**Shopping Hints:**          **Price range: ¥80–¥200 per dose**
—A 20 day supply of powdered horse teeth to cure
rheumatism is only ¥2,000. A monkey's head, available
charred and whole but taken in powdered form, is ¥6,000—
the perfect gift for the person who has everything, including
brain disease or mental disorder. Also available are praying
mantis to cure infected wounds, earthworms to alleviate fever
and bees' nests to stimulate mother's milk.
—You might prefer a cold cure of fragrant roots and bark. It
should be brewed for 30 minutes and drunk as a strong tea.

# Kyoya

12-10 Ueno 2-chome Taito-ku.    Tel. 831-1905.
**Hours:** 9:30–7:30 (Closed Sun.).    Founded 1912.
**Specialty:** traditional nail-less furniture (*sashimono*).
Owner: Yasuno Takao (plus 6 employees and 13 part-time craftsmen).

Three generations ago Takao-san, who had been selling cabinets from a hand-pulled cart, opened a small shop. Soon afterwards he exhibited cabinets of *kuwa* (mulberry) at a fair held in Ueno Park, and the unusual cabinets brought him national fame. Today KYOYA is known throughout Japan as the only shop producing Edo-style furnishings. The shop still favors *kuwa* with its splendidly patterned grain but also uses pine, cedar, walnut and the popular *kiri* (paulownia). Lightweight *kiri* is frequently used for *tansu*, chests of drawers made in several stackable sections.

The traditional furniture of *kanto*, the northern part of Japan, and *kansai*, the southern part, reveal regional differences of taste. *Kansai* pieces are often thickly lacquered and decorated with paintings. *Kanto* families preferred to live with natural or polished woods whose grain and texture remained visible. Tokyo merchants were devotees of cabinets with many secret drawers and hidden locks.

**Shopping Hints:**    **Price range: ¥5,000–¥1,000,000**

—Two styles of *tansu* may be ordered at KYOYA: *tansu* of very plain *kiri*, and *sendai-dansu* which are ornate and polished or lacquered. *Sendai-dansu* originated as small chests for storage on ships but are now ordered in larger sizes by many foreigners. From ¥300,000 to ¥1,000,000.

—A copper-lined tobacco box (*hai-otoshi*) costs ¥13,000.

—A sewing box with elevated pin cushion and drawers (*haribako*) costs ¥33,000. (Order one month in advance.)

—Letter boxes (*fumibako*) lined with hand-made paper are ¥5,000 to ¥6,000.

—*Andon*, the portable standing lanterns of Edo times, are ¥20,000 to ¥50,000. Tables, standing mirrors, tea trays, and wooden tea saucers are also available.

# Sairaku-do

18-1 Ueno 1-chome Taito-ku.      Tel. 832-0024.
**Hours:** 10: 00–6: 00 (Closed Sun. and Hols.).      Founded 1925.
**Specialty:** wood block prints (*ukiyo-e*).
Owner: Saiju Nishi (plus wife).

Once surrounded by antique dealers, SAIRAKU-DO is left alone today with its business of buying and selling woodblock prints. The father of the present owner was a rice wholesaler who collected *ukiyo-e* prints as a hobby. The hobby became a consuming interest, and he opened a shop in 1925. Today SAIRAKU-DO has original prints and copies, but it is a shop for experienced collectors only. You must know what to ask for.

*Ukiyo-e* are categorized by subject matter. *Bijin-ga* are beauty portraits of women, *yakusha-e* are prints of actors and other famous people, and *fuzoku* depict scenery or the life of the city. *Bijin-ga* are considered the most difficult to make; one should note the thin strands of hair, the colors, the shading techniques and the translucency of the cloth.

The best *ukiyo-e* date from the later Edo Period and the beginning of the Meiji Period. Usually 300 prints were made, often for posters publicizing an actor or shop. At the time they were not thought to have much artistic merit and frugal merchants often used them as wrapping material, for the hand-made *washi* paper on which they were printed was very strong. European importers sometimes found an unexpected esthetic bonus in their shipments of tea from Japan. The appreciation of *ukiyo-e* prints began in Europe where they had considerable influence on the Impressionists.

Good originals are still occasionally found in towns on the Japan Sea which had once been prosperous ports.

**Shopping Hints:**      **Price range: ¥1,000–¥10,000,000**
—Prices for original prints range between ¥10,000 and ¥10,000,000.
—The price of recent copies depends on the size of the print. *Ohban*, the largest, is ¥3,000; *chuban*, medium-sized, is ¥1,500; *futatsu-giri*, the smallest, is ¥1,000.

# Usagi-ya

10-10 Ueno 1-chome Taito-ku.    Tel. 831-6195.
**Hours:** 9:00–6:00 (Closed Wed.).    Founded 1913.
**Specialty:** sweet tea cakes (*wa-gashi*).
Owner: Shotaro Taniguchi (plus 3 sons and 30 employees).

A white china rabbit crouching on the roof honors the name of the shop (*usagi* means rabbit) and signifies the year of birth of its founder 3 generations ago. Taniguchi-san was a colorful character who had been a banker and a candle dealer. He began to sell rice crackers and sweet bean-cakes to customers of geisha houses, attracting their amused attention by giving the cakes his own first name. His wit helped him prosper, and in 1913 he opened a shop. His son who loved *haiku* poetry brought many Ueno artists and writers to USAGI-YA; the calligraphy displayed on the walls were gifts from these men.

The customer at USAGI-YA looks at the samples set out on pottery plates along the display counter and gives the proprietor his order. The order is called out to the back of the shop where, unseen, the freshly made sweets are attractively wrapped. The shop's two specialties are *kisaku-monaka* and *dorayaki*. The first is a round, dry wafer filled with sweet bean paste; the second looks like a pancake filled with dark bean jam. About 30 other kinds of cakes are also available, almost all of which contain a filling of sweet beans or soft rice. They are most delicious when eaten soon after they are made. After 4 or 5 hours they become a bit dry and less flavorful.

**Shopping Hints:**    Price range: ¥25–¥5,000
—*Kisaku-monaka* are ¥35 each, or ¥390 for a gift box of 10. *Dorayaki* are ¥70 each, or ¥770 for a gift box of 10.
—In the spring try *sakura-mochi*, a delicate pink sweet wrapped in a deliciously pickled cherry leaf, and *kusa-mochi*, a green rice cake flavored with a delicious and fragrant kind of grass.
—*Jo-nama-gashi*, the most expensive cakes, change seasonally. *Momo* (peach) is for early spring, *tsubaki* (camellia) is for spring, and *neko-yanagi* (pussy willow) is for early summer.

# ASAKUSABASHI

North from Asakusabashi bridge stretches the highway to Sendai and other cities of northern Japan. One hundred years ago, travelers approaching Tokyo knew that their journey was ending when the broad, open avenue became lined with street-stalls selling dolls and toys. Today many doll and toy wholesalers are still located on this busy street, but their open-air stalls have moved indoors into modern glass and steel buildings.

Strictly speaking, Asakusabashi is the small area directly north of the train station on the Sobu Line; but in common parlance, Yanagibashi and Kuramae are also included within its boundaries.

Yanagibashi is famous for its many expensive Japanese restaurants and for its geisha. Under the tracks of the Sobu Line you can see a small shop from which *jinrikisha* are dispatched each night to take the geisha from their homes to one of the 16 restaurants in Asakusabashi where their services have been requested. To reserve a geisha, the host of a party calls the central geisha office, or *kenban*, which then contacts as many of the 80 Yanagibashi geisha as are needed. Today almost all the geisha live in their own *manshon* (apartments), but in pre-war days small groups of them lived in homes, called *okiya*, presided over by a retired geisha.

The Sumida River running past Yanagibashi is important to community life. In past centuries, geisha often entertained on pleasure boats floating along the river (see KOMATSU-YA, p. 48.). A river-opening festival of fireworks, *Ryogoku kawabiraki*, is still held in the middle of July near the Ryogokubashi bridge. Another festival, *Toroh nagashi*, during which candles set in small lanterns are floated out to sea, is held at the end of August. People whose livelihood depends on the river offer these lanterns to thank the Sumida for its gifts.

Formerly the *sumo* stadium, Kokugi-kan, was located across the Ryogokubashi bridge, but after the war a newer and bigger stadium was built in Kuramae. Many of the Yanagibashi geisha are fans of the *sumo* wrestlers.

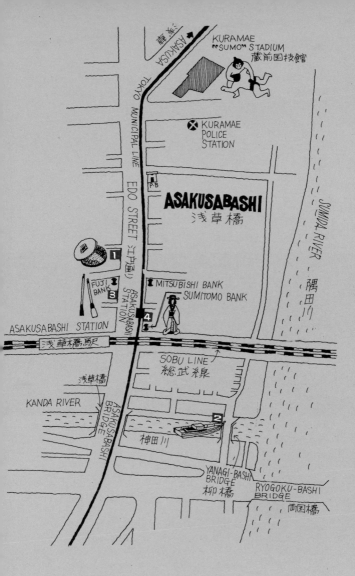

1. **Funasa** 鮒 佐（江戸通り西側）⇨pp. 46 & 47.
2. **Komatsu-ya** 小 松 屋（柳橋たもと）⇨pp. 48 & 49.
3. **Koun-do** 光 雲 堂（久月斜め向い）⇨pp. 50 & 51.
4. **Kyugetsu** 久 月（住友銀行隣）⇨pp. 52 & 53.

# Funasa

1-9 Asakusabashi 2-chome Taito-ku.    Tel. 851-7710.
**Hours:** 9: 00–5: 30 (Closed Sun. and Hols.).    Founded 1856.
**Specialty:** small seasoned fish and shellfish (*tsukudani*).
Owner: Sakichi Ohno (plus 4 employees).


*Tsukudani* originated in a district on Tokyo Bay known as Tsukudajima where tiny fish were boiled in a richly seasoned sauce until most of the liquid had evaporated and the fish had a thick, dark, lustrous coating. A local peddler brought *tsukudani* to Edo, selling them in the old Nihonbashi fish-market area. Their salty taste and high preservability gained them immediate popularity.

FUNASA was founded by Sohbei Ohno who was intrigued with the small fish delicacies from Tsukudajima and loved to experiment with ways of improving their preparation. His shop was the first to make and sell the seasoned fish under the name *tsukudani*, which means boiled island products. The shop is well known and at least once has received literary recognition when, in the classic Meiji novel *Onnakeizu*, a famous geisha brings to the heroine a gift of "*Funasa-no-tsukudani*."

Three kinds of *tsukudani* are sold in Tokyo today: the original Tsukudajima style in which tiny white fish are cooked in special soy sauce; Aomori Prefecture style in which unshelled shrimp are boiled in a sweet sauce; and *shigure* style in which clams are cooked in a thick, fermented soy sauce. *Tsukudani* accompany breakfast rice, appear in *obento*, lunchboxes and are mixed with tea and rice in the dish called *ocha-zuke*.

**Shopping Hints:**        **Price range: ¥450–¥6,500**
—*Magemono*, round, shallow wooden gift boxes with an assortment of *tsukudani*, are priced at ¥450 to ¥6,500. If you would like an assortment for yourself without the gift box, you may say, "*mazete-tsukutte-kudasai*." The price will be ¥500.
—Ordered individually in 200 gram containers, *anago* (sea eel) costs ¥1,400; *shirasu* and *ebi* (tiny white fish and shrimp) are ¥800; *asari*, *gobo* and *haze* (shellfish, burdock root and goby) are ¥800; *kombu* (seaweed) is ¥400.

# Komatsu-ya

2-1 Yanagibashi 1-chome Taito-ku.    Tel. 851-2783.
**Hours:** 9 : 00–7 : 00 (Closed Sun.).    Founded 1913.
**Specialty:** boat rental (*funayado*).
Owner: Isao Akimoto (plus 6 employees).

In front of KOMATSU-YA is a bold, standing banner right out of the 16th century when feudal lords unfurled family banners on boats not so different from those you see here. In the 17th century more and more nobles and Edo merchants began to hold lavish parties on boats like these. To take care of the demand, a special catering service developed—the *funayado* house that rented boats and provided food, geisha and other entertainers. These pleasure boats, called *yakata-bune*, could still be seen on the Sumida River as recently as 10 years ago. Restaurants fitted out some of the best ones, and *kabuki* and movie actors were among their regular customers.

The founder of KOMATSU-YA hoped to establish a business based on the old *yakata-bune* customs, but today his son rents only boats for fishing. He also sells delicious fish tidbits prepared in his tiny shop perched over the Sumida River. Perhaps someday, he muses, pollution will be halted, and leisurely evenings on pleasure boats will once again be possible.

**Shopping Hints:**        **Price range: ¥1,000–¥40,000**
—Each of KOMATSU-YA's 5 boats is provided with an oarsman and guide who also prepares a tempura lunch on board. The price is ¥50,000 a day for a party of 10.
—The specialty of the shop is *suzume-yaki*, an hors d'oeuvre of tiny crucian carp grilled over charcoal and seasoned with sweet soy sauce; ¥55 a skewer. Two other delicacies are *onigara-yaki*, charcoal-broiled seasoned shrimp heads, and *hito-kuchi-anago*, sea-eel seasoned with soy sauce and sugar.
—Be sure to look at the old house across the river from the boat-house. Now the family home, it was once an inn for fisherman-guests.

49

# Koh-un-do

30-11 Asakusabashi 1-chome Taito-ku.     Tel 861-4943.
**Hours:** 9: 00–5: 00 (Closed Sun. and Hols.).     Founded 1793.
**Specialty:** writing brushes (*fude*).
Owner: Zensuke Ohtani (plus 9 employees).

Three giant sample brushes hang in the middle of the
shop and over 300 kinds of brushes fill its shelves. Two of
Tokyo's best brushmakers, one of them a 4th generation
maker of brush-tips, work for KOH-UN-DO producing
*mizu-fude*, a kind of brush developed in the 11th century.
To make *mizu-fude* the hairs are boiled to remove the oil,
dried and matched by length and thickness. Then, one by
one, the imperfect hairs are removed by hand. Finally tiny
bunches of different lengths are grouped together by a
complicated process of pasting and folding until the
bunches are well mixed. Ohtani-san explains that it takes
15 years to master the art of making *mizu-fude*.

Over 200 kinds of hair are used in making *fude* tips.
Light brown weasel is used for fine lettering brushes. For
large lettering, there are thick tapered brushes of white
wool. Brushes made of cat hair, which is wider at the tip
and thus holds the ink well, are used for painting designs on
lacquerware and the faces on dolls. Squirrel, deer, dog,
racoon and horse hair have all been used for *fude* in the
past. The fine bamboo handles for KOH-UN-DO's
brushes come from Hyogo Prefecture where the bamboo is
boiled, scrubbed, bleached and polished before being
fitted with the brush tip.

Writing brushes came to Japan from China in the 8th
century. Seventeen of these very early brushes are kept as
National Treasures in the Imperial Repository in Nara.

**Shopping Hints:**                **Price range: ¥400–¥130,000**
—A medium-size brush (*kanji-fude*) costs from ¥500 to ¥2,000
and a small brush (*kana-fude*) is ¥500 to ¥700.
—An elegant peacock-feather brush, called *kujaku-fude*, is used
in modern "abstract" calligraphy.
—*Fude-kake*, a small bamboo rack on which brushes are hung,
costs ¥5,000.

51

# Kyugetsu

Map (p. 45, Asakusabashi #4)

20-4 Yanagibashi 1-chome Taito-ku.    Tel. 861-5511.
**Hours:** 9:00–5:00 (From Jan. to May, open every day. From May to Dec., closed Sun. and Hols.).    Founded 1830.
**Specialty:** dolls (*ningyo*).
Owner: Kakuro Yokoyama (plus 150 employees).

At KYUGETSU you will see *noh* and *kabuki* char-actor dolls, pottery dolls from Hakata and even modern French-style dolls. There are special dolls called *hina-ningyo* for Girls' Day on March 3; and there are boy dolls, helmets and armor for Children's Day on May 5 (formerly known as Boys' Day). These festival dolls go on sale 2 months ahead of time and fill the first floor of the store.

The founder of KYUGETSU was Kyuzaemon Yoko-yama, said to be a descendant of the Emperor Seiwa, an ancestor of the Genji clan. Yokoyama-san made *hina*-doll sets and wooden tops, and he supplied many street-sellers with dolls for the popular Asakusabashi fairs that preceded the Girls' and Boys' Day festivals.

Originally Japanese dolls were symbolic images of gods and humans and were meant as protective charms. Mini-ature dolls became popular with girls of the aristocracy in the 11th century, and displaying dolls became part of the spring festival for girls in the Edo Period. At the end of the Edo Period, dolls with movable parts and with the face modelled after a famous *kabuki* actor, Sano Ichimatsu, became popular as toys. The Ichimatsu doll was a favorite till the end of World War II.

**Shopping Hints:**          **Price range: ¥800–¥3,000,000**
—The two major types of Girls' Day *hina-ningyo* are the realistic *ishogi* and the stylized *kimekomi*. They may be bought as the prince and princess pair or as a complete set of 15 dolls, with or without a glass case. From ¥25,000 to ¥1,500,000. Ornamental helmets for Children's Day are ¥6,000 to ¥1,000,000.
—*Musume-dojoji*, depicting a traditional dance, is ¥5,000.
—The appealing *haiko-ningyo*, a crawling baby doll with movable head, arms and legs, is ¥1,600.

# NINGYO-CHO

The settlement of Ningyo-cho began in the 17th century when the Tokugawa *shogun* first came to Edo to establish his domain. A group of doll and *bunraku* puppet makers moved into one part of the area, and as early as 1692 a map was drawn up naming the district after these puppet and doll (*ningyo*) craftsmen.

Yoshiwara, the famed red-light district, was established in the area in 1617 to provide entertainment for the many laborers who had been brought in from the country by the *shogun* to work on land-reclamation projects. Soon the Yoshiwara began to overflow the confines of its Sumida River boundary, and when a great fire in 1657 destroyed almost all of its buildings, it was removed to Asakusa where remnants remain today.

Just north of Ningyo-cho is the section called Shibai-machi (theater town). It was a center for *kabuki* drama and other forms of popular entertainment until the end of the Edo Period. East of Ningyo-cho is the Meiji-za Theater, modern in appearance, but established in 1893 by a famous *kabuki* actor. For many years it presented only *kabuki* drama, but today its fame rests on *shimpa* and *shinkokugeki*, relatively modern plays performed seasonally.

A park, Hama-cho Koen, near the Meiji-za and at the edge of the Sumida River, was once frequented by romantic boaters. Today it is a popular place for summer *bon-odori*, informal community dancing. Geisha who live in the area often participate in the *bon-odori*; a group of these geisha, *kurenai-kai*, presents a dance recital each spring at the Meiji-za.

A famous shrine in the area, Suiten-gu, is an appropriate place to pray for deliverance from disaster by fire or water. Expectant mothers should go there to pray for an easy birth.

# NINGYO-CHO
## 人形町

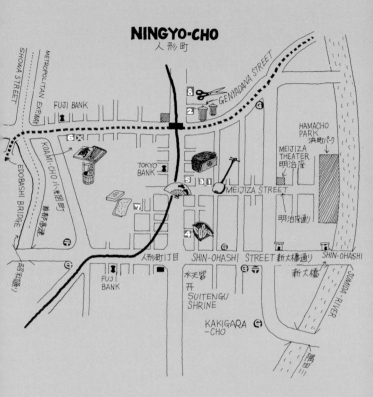

55

# Bachi-Ei Map (p. 55, Ningyo-cho #1)

14 Ningyo-cho 2-chome Nihonbashi Chuo-ku.    Tel. 666-7263.
**Hours:** 9: 30–9: 00 (Closed Sun. and Hols.).    Founded 1893.
**Specialty:** *shamisen.*
Owner: Eijiro Kobayashi (plus 2 employees).

Entering the tiny workshop, you may see an elaborate peg frame stretching a recently applied skin over a new *shamisen* sound box. In the winter or rainy season the frame is often suspended over a charcoal brazier to speed the drying process. BACHI-EI is one of Tokyo's 27 shops which make the entire *shamisen* instrument.

Near the turn of the century many *samurai,* among whom was the grandfather of today's proprietor, found themselves without occupation. Establishing himself first as a maker of the *shamisen* pick, his shop later began to produce the complete instrument. The three-stringed *shamisen*, introduced to Japan from Okinawa, greatly influenced the development of puppet plays in the 1500's and *kabuki* drama, as well as all schools of Japanese singing. It is still commonly used today in many art and entertainment forms.

At BACHI-EI Kobayashi-san makes and sells two kinds of *shamisen: chu-zao* and *hoso-zao* (medium- and narrow-necked styles). Rosewood or Chinese quince, which must be dried for at least a year, is used to make the four pieces of the *shamisen* body, and cat or dog skin is used to cover the two sides of the sound box. Cat is preferred and is more expensive. The large, spatula-like *shamisen* pick is called *bachi* and is made from wood for practice, or from plastic, tortoise shell or ivory for performance use.

Usually the *shamisen* is kept upright on a special stand or is hung from a kind of frame on the wall, but the four pieces and padded edge cover are easily disassembled to fit into a special briefcase for modern carrying convenience.

**Shopping Hints:**          **Price range: ¥35,000–¥300,000**
—An inexpensive *shamisen* can be bought for about ¥35,000 and a medium price one for ¥100,000.
—A set of 3 silk strings of various widths is ¥140.

# Iseryu
Map (p. 55, Ningyo-cho #2)

2 Ningyo-cho 3-chome Nihonbashi Chuo-ku.     Tel. 661-4820.
**Hours:** 8: 00–6: 00 (Closed Sun. and Hols.).     Founded 1873.
**Specialty:** everyday dishes (*seto-mono*).
Owner: Ryutaro Itoh (plus wife and 4 employees).

Teapots suspended from the ceiling; rice bowls, teacups and small dishes of many shapes stacked on shelves with branch supports; the earthen floor which protects a falling dish—all give the impression of a comfortable old neighborhood shop. Located on the same site for 100 years, ISERYU was once the neighbor of a famous *rakugo* theater and of an old row-house said to be the home of Otomi-san, a colorful woman about whom a *kabuki* drama was written.

ISERYU features everday chinaware from Seto (Aichi Prefecture), and a few more expensive items from Kiyomizu (Kyoto) and Kutani (Ishikawa Prefecture). Japanese dishes, *not* meant to match, are wonderfully specialized with tiny saucers for soy sauce or pickles, rectangular plates for fish, and appropriate shapes and sizes of bowls for rice, raw fish, vegetables and soups, all of which are selected by the housewife to create an artful arrangement of their delicious contents. However, a few types of dishes, some teapots and cups do come in matching sets, in which case there are always five to a set.

There are two categories of teapots: *dobin*, with the familiar, half-circle attached handle (usually bamboo), and *kyusu*, with a projecting handle made from the same material as the pot. You might look at ISERYU's display of large cups called *Hyakunin-isshu* which are decorated on the outside with court lords and ladies and on the inside, incredibly, each with 100 poems. These antiques are not for sale, but are part of the Itoh family heirlooms.

**Shopping Hints:**     **Price range: ￥100–￥35,000**
—An individual teacup may be purchased for as little as ￥150, a rice bowl for ￥100 and a vase for between ￥150–￥35,000.
—*Dobin* are ￥500–￥3,000, and *kyusu* are ￥500–￥8,000.

# Iwai-shoten Map (p. 55, Ningyo-cho #3).

14 Ningyo-cho 2-chome Nihonbashi Chuo-ku.     Tel. 668-6058.
**Hours:** 9: 00–6: 00 (Closed New Year's).     Founded 1863.
**Specialty:** lacquered bamboo trunks (*tsuzura*).
Owner: Taichi Iwai (plus wife).

Bamboo baskets in various stages of the covering process can be seen hung from the ceiling of this modest shop or stacked out on the street to dry in the sun. Pots of lacquer and piles of hand-made paper are in one corner of the room.

Long ago these storage trunks were an essential household item. Today, however, they are ordered only by special segments of Japanese society, particularly theatrical people and geisha. Traditionally they were indispensable in transporting the clothing and posessions of feudal lords, and even today they are still used in some parts of Japan as a hope chest transported ceremoniously to the bride's new home.

Iwai-san, a fourth generation *tsuzura* maker, uses wide-weave bamboo baskets made on Sado Island. Two layers of thin, used, hand-made paper (old documents obtained from government offices) are applied to the outside with a flour-and-water paste. This is covered with a chemical lacquer, by tradition black, dark brown or orange. The edges are reinforced and the insides lined with two other kinds of paper. *Tsuzura* are made to order and are decorated with the family crest. The first name of the owner is often written on one side of the lid.

A good *tsuzura* will last a lifetime, and Iwai-san is frequently called on to repair (soak off the lacquered paper and refinish) fine old trunks which have been handed down through several generations.

**Shopping Hints:**     **Price range: ¥1,900–¥11,500**
—*Tsuzura* must be ordered, but if you are lucky they might have an extra one for immediate sale: *Tebunko*, small size (for letters), ¥1,900; *Kake-go*, medium size (for *tabi* and undergarments), ¥5,500; *Tsuzura*, large size (for storing *kimono*, *obi*, etc.) ¥11,500.

# Kotobuki-do

2-4 Ningyo-cho 1-chome Nihonbashi Chuo-ku.
Tel. 666-4804.
**Hours:** 9: 00–10: 00 (Weekdays), 10: 00–6: 00 (Sun.).
**Specialty:** tea sweets (*wa-gashi*).      Founded 1883.
Owner: Hirokazu Sugiyama (plus mother and 6 employees).

This tiny shop with its elegant window display of fresh cakes and candies arranged on beautiful antique plates or in old lacquered boxes has recently been the inspiration for an evening NHK-TV drama series.

Sugiyama-san's grandfather opened his shop in Kyoto and developed a way of making *kogane-imo*, golden yam cakes, a tea pastry made with white beans covered with cinnamon. These cakes gained great popularity, and there was a time when even the Imperial Family were customers. Former Prime Minister Sato, another famous customer, brought these cakes as his gift on one formal state occasion.

Today, besides the *kogane-imo* a variety of delicious and beautiful cakes and candies are available. There are three categories of tea sweets: *higashi*, dry, brittle, tiny elaborate candies; *han-namagashi*, half-soft, gumdrop-like candies; and *namagashi*, soft, larger sweets often made with various kinds of bean fillings.

In tea sweets, as in *haiku* poems and other expressions of Japanese culture, an awareness of the seasons is important. You might ask the family to point out a framed list of tea sweets used 70 years ago which specifies the appropriate types of cakes and candies made by KOTOBUKI-DO during the spring, summer, autumn and winter.

**Shopping Hints:**          **Price range: ¥20–¥2,500**
—A popular gift assortment of *kogane-imo* is available at ¥770; however, you may buy any number of these cakes at ¥70 each.
—A delightful candy made of sugar-coated sesame seed and packaged as a straw rice bundle is available in 3 sizes, beginning at ¥250. Called *yojoto*, this is an ancient health food. Ask for *tawara-gashi*.

# Kyosen-do Map (p. 55, Ningyo-cho #5)

2 Ningyo-cho 2-chome Nihonbashi Chuo-ku.     Tel. 666-7255.
**Hours:** 10: 00–6: 00 (Closed Sun. and Hols.).     Founded 1833.
**Specialty:** fans (*sensu*). Owner: Shunsaku Saiki (plus son, 1
employee and 23 employees at Kyoto factory).


KYOSEN-DO was first established in Kyoto by a
Buddhist monk who learned from temple elders the art of
making traditional ceremonial fans. Originally limited to
religious worship, fans have had great importance throughout Japanese history. During the 7th century fans began to
be used at all formal and ceremonial occasions. Symbolic
of respect and good will, they are appropriate gifts to
friends and family on special days.

The size, shape and design of a fan determine its use.
There are two fan styles: folding fans, *sensu* or *ohgi*,
for formal and ceremonial use; and flat fans, *uchiwa*,
used in the kitchen for fanning the fire or on hot summer
days. Except for a few miniature flat fans, KYOSEN-DO
deals only in *sensu* made of bamboo and hand-made paper
by Kyoto craftsmen. Designs are printed on most fans.
Only the most expensive are hand-painted; these are often
considered art objects for display rather than use.

Do notice the full size copy (¥15,000) of the strung fan
used by the Empress and court ladies and often seen in
miniature in elaborate Girls' Day Festival sets.

**Shopping Hints:**          **Price range: ¥150–¥15,000**
—Religious fans used by Buddhist priests are large, Y-shaped,
   only ¼ open. *Noh* drama and dance fans are large, have 10
   ribs and a V-angle steeper than others. *Kabuki* drama and
   dance fans are large with 10 ribs and often with a large design
   to be seen from the stage. Tea ceremony fans are small, carried tucked in the *obi*, rarely opened. Fans used by students
   of Sutra chanting are dark blue or black, covered with Sutra
   prayers. Summer fans are usually of paper, but some for
   women are made of silk.
—The miniature fans are for decorative use.
—Miniature sets of fan and tea bowl, vase, etc., are given as
   wedding favors and return baby gifts.

1 Koami-cho 1-chome Nihonbashi Chuo-ku.     Tel. 666-3906.
**Hours:** 9: 00–5: 00 (Closed Sun. and Hols.).     Founded 1704.
**Specialty:** toothpicks (*yōji*).
Owner: Hichirobei Yamamoto (plus 43 employees).


Seven generations ago, Yamamoto-san, a street enter-
tainer with a pet monkey, *saru*, strolled about on New
Year's Day selling the customary gift toothpicks. His
great-grandson added a variation to the family business—a
poetic fortune wrapped around each toothpick. The
fortunes were so popular that he opened a shop later
immortalized in a series of prints by Kuniyoshi in *ukiyo-e*
style.

Two categories of picks are made and sold at SARU-
YA: *tsuma-yoji* for teeth; and *kashi-yoji*, a longer style
used for cutting and eating tea sweets. The best picks are
made of *kuromoji*, a small tree of the camphor species.
They are cut by hand into a distinctive shape with an
attractive strip of bark on one side. These picks are
somewhat expensive as most of the center white wood of
each tree is wasted. Cheaper toothpicks are made by
machine from the wood of white birch and do not have
the esthetically important strips of dark bark.

SARU-YA, has become the distributor for toothpicks
and cake picks throughout Japan. They are frequently
sold in department stores, and gift packages continue to
be popular presents during the New Year season.

**Shopping Hints:**          Price range: ¥50–¥2,600
—Be sure to take home a package of *kiri-bako-iri*, toothpicks
  wrapped with a red tipped fortune-like poem, frequently with
  a suggestive connotation. (A ¥300 box is recommended.)
—Other gifts include toothpick stands and holders, a tiny
  toothpick carrying case, a minuscule tortoise-shell ear cleaner
  in an attractive case, folding purses, calling card and
  cigarette cases, pocket combs and mirrors all made with
  traditional Japanese paper. A catalogue is available.
—For ¥24,500 you can order 5,000 toothpicks with your name
  printed on each paper pick wrapping.

# Takayanagi Shokuhin    Map (p. 55, Ningyo-cho #7)

11-2 Kakigara-cho 2-chome Chuo-ku.    Tel. 666-2608.
**Hours:** 9: 00–6: 00 (Closed Sun, and Hols.).    Founded 1913.
**Specialty:** soybean curd (*tofu*).
Owner: Asao Takayanagi (plus two sons and daughter).

You can't eat Japanese food for long without meeting *tofu*. Small cubes of it floating in the breakfast soup; a cold block topped with grated ginger on a hot summer day; squares of it in *sukiyaki* and *mizutaki*—the list goes on and on. High in protein, *tofu* is becoming internationally known as an ideal food. (Health-food lovers might like to try *tohnyu*, a by-product of *tofu*-making hard to find outside Japan. Warm it up and mix with a little honey.)

Every day *tofu* is made in countless neighborhood shops all over Japan. At TAKAYANAGI-SHOKUHIN the entire process can be watched. Each morning Takayanagi-san grinds the soybeans which have been soaking overnight and simmers them for two hours in an enormous copper kettle. A "milk" is produced which is filtered through cotton cloth to remove the lee (sold as a rich feed for animals), and a brine is added as a solidifier. After draining for about 20 minutes, the finished block is placed in a tank of water and cut into small blocks.

Many housewives bring their own containers to the *tofu* shop, as their mothers and grandmothers used to do. They find the *tofu* sold by supermarkets in prepackaged plastic containers far less delicious than Takayanagi-san's *tofu* freshly made each day in the old-fashioned way his grandfather taught him.

**Shopping Hints:**              **Price range: ¥25–¥50**
—*Tofu* comes in many forms: *momen-dofu* is the basic kind; one block is called *it-cho*, two *ni-cho*, etc. *Kinu-goshi-dofu* has a very smooth texture (*kinu*=silk). *Yaki-dofu* is broiled on top for firmness and flavor. *Age* is deep-fried and thinly sliced; *nama-age* is also deep-fried, but in block-form. *Gan-modoki* is a fried patty of *tofu* and bits of vegetables.
—Do ask for some *age-no-dekitate*, fried *tofu* hot out of the pan. A crispy snack, delicious dipped in soy sauce.

# Ubuke-ya

Map (p. 55, Ningyo-cho #8)

4 Ningyo-cho 3-chome, Nihonbashi Chuo-ku.    Tel. 661–4851.
**Hours:** 9:00–6:30 (Closed Sun.).    Founded 1793.
**Specialty:** tweezers, scisssors (*kenuki, hasami*).
Owner: Hideo Yazaki (plus wife).


Of all the shops in Ningyo-cho, the modest UBUKE-YA has certainly the loveliest interior, a truly fine example of old Edo elegance and simplicity. The lady may purchase traditional tweezers for the removal of inverted eyelashes, or she may choose from a variety of pinch-type Japanese scissors, western scissors, knives or nail cutters. Professional hand tools are also available.

UBUKE-YA opened in Osaka and moved to Tokyo during the Meiji Restoration. Tweezers, in the past, were an important household item used not only for beauty purposes but also for a variety of specific daily tasks: the removal of small bones in fish fillets, picking off unwanted threads, taking out thorns and splinters, etc. Lamentably, the variety of tweezers has been reduced to two: *toge-nuki* for removing thorns, and *matsuge-nuki* for those inverted eyelashes.

Three craftsmen are employed to make scissors, and all are descendants of Yakichi Yoshida, the first maker of Western-style scissors in Japan some 90 years ago. One pair of large, early Meiji scissors made by Yoshida-san is still displayed in a case over the counter.

The fame of UBUKE-YA has spread by word of mouth, and it is even mentioned by name in the well-known *rakugo* story "Dogu-ya." (At one time the famous *rakugo* theater, Suehiro Tei, was located next to this shop.)


**Shopping Hints:**    Price range: ¥600–¥9,500
—Tweezers are available at ¥600 and ¥800.
—*Tachi-basami* (Western scissors) come in 2 sizes. There are *nigiri-basami* (Japanese scissors) for finger nails, silk thread, cloth or general use.
—*Hana-basami*, *ueki-basami* and *bonsai-basami* (flower, hedge and miniature tree clippers) are available.

# NIHONBASHI

Over a wide, clear river lined with pines, Nihonbashi bridge was constructed in 1603. A year later a stone marker at the bridge became the point from which distances throughout the entire country were measured, and from this spot originated 5 main roads which radiated out to all parts of Japan. Today there is a newer stone marker on the north side of the bridge.

After the construction of the bridge, Nihonbashi became the central shopping and business area of Tokyo. The central fish market was established near the bridge (this market was later moved to Tsukiji), and shops dealing in fish products, dried foods and many other articles grew up around it. Money changers handling the many currencies from the different regions of Japan settled in Nihonbashi; these were the predecessors of the major banks which now have their headquarters here.

As Nihonbashi prospered, it became the center for public announcements; traditionally all journeys originated from its bridge. Journeys in those days were plentiful and spectacular, for by government decree all feudal lords had to pay bi-yearly visits to the capital. (Also by government decree, the wives and children of the lords were established in Edo residences—magnificent places whose upkeep contributed to the wealth of the city, kept the *daimyo* lords suitably short of funds and guaranteed their periodic appearance in the city.) The pageantry of the processions of ruling *daimyos* passing through the beautiful countryside and over the bridge is still remembered in the nostalgic song, "O-Edo Nihonbashi."

The fiery, gay, generous and mercurial spirit of today's *Edokko* (a 3rd-generation resident of Tokyo) is said to have originated around this downtown Nihonbashi district.

# Benmatsu

Map (p. 73, Nihonbashi #1)

16 Muro-machi 1-chome Nihonbashi Chuo-ku.     Tel. 279-2361.
**Hours:** 9: 30–5: 00 (Closed Mon.).     Founded 1850.
**Specialty:** box lunches (*orizume*).
Owner: Tetsuro Higuchi (plus 18 employees).

Come to BENMATSU in the morning, and you will be
greeted by a delicious aroma from trays heaped with
tempting pieces of grilled fish, spiced vegetables, bamboo
shoots and more. Beautifully arranged in box lunches,
these foods are enjoyed by workmen, businessmen, dance
recital guests and families on outings.

The first Higuchi-san of BENMATSU opened a small
restaurant popular with fish sellers from the old central
marketplace. He was, however, dismayed to find his customers so busy that they frequently hurried off leaving
rice and bits of food behind, and so he began to pack
lunches in small boxes for them to carry back to work.
Becoming well known for this service, BENMATSU
eventually abandoned its tables and devoted itself entirely
to the box lunches. The first Higuchi-san is credited with
inventing the very popular Japanese picnic lunch called
*orizume*. (The photo on the next page shows a selection of
these.)

BENMATSU makes about 700 or 800 lunches a day. A
record sale of several thousand lunches occurred in 1905
on the day Japan won the war against Russia. Many
residents of Tokyo bought box lunches to carry into the
streets while celebrating the victory.

**Shopping Hints:**     **Price range: ¥350–¥5,000**
Order a day or more ahead. There are set assortments at different prices:
—Rice, vegetables, omelet, pickles, a prawn or two and
  *kamaboko* (fish-cake slices), for ¥300.
—Rice, chestnuts, fish teriyaki, vegetables, omelet, *kamaboko*
  and pickles for ¥450.
—An assortment for 3 people includes all of the above foods
  plus squid, stuffed *tofu* (soy bean curd), mushrooms, shrimp,
  lotus root and octopus, for ¥5,000.

## Fujiwara Obiji-ten    Map (p. 73, Nihonbashi #2)

2-8 Nihonbashi 2-chome Chuo-ku.    Tel. 271-1785.
**Hours:** 9:00–6:00 (Closed Sun.).    Founded 1913.
**Specialty:** women's sashes (*obi*).
Owner: Hiroyuki Fujiwara (plus 13 employees).

The customer kneels politely on the *tatami* and waits to be shown a selection of *obi* sashes. In FUJIWARA OBIJI-TEN you will find only pure silk *obi*, for Fujiwara-san considers synthetic material uncomfortable and of inferior quality.

The origins of this shop lie in Kyoto where a century ago the first Fujiwara-san peddled sashes from door-to-door. An imaginative man, he adapted *Noh* drama designs for use on his *obi*. The idea caught on, and he became so prosperous that he opened a shop in Tokyo and a weaving establishment back in Kyoto to supply his shop with material. Before World War II, FUJIWARA OBIJI-TEN made many *obi* for the Imperial Family. During the war the shop's 15 looms were turned over to the government for scrap metal. Since then it has obtained its *obi* from one of the finest weaving concerns in Kyoto.

The history of the *obi* goes back to the 8th century when sashes of woven cloth began to take the place of hemp cords for tying up kimono. In the 1400's women's sashes became different from men's—wider and more decorative. Traditionally they have been the chief adornment of a Japanese woman's costume, the equivalent of a Western woman's jewels.

**Shopping Hints:**    **Price range: ¥7,000–¥6,000,000**
—*Maru-obi* are 60 cm. wide (2 ft.); of silk brocade with the design running the entire length; the most expensive. *Fukuro-obi* are also wide and long with the design in 2 or 3 places. *Nagoya-obi* are easy to tie and inexpensive, prefolded at one end with the design in 3 places. To wear all of these, fold so that the front measures 15 cm. (6 inches).
—*Odori-obi* are narrower than the three above; colorful designs, for children and Japanese dancers. *Kaku-obi* are narrow and dark; used by men. *Hakata-obi* are used by women in the summer and by men anytime; usually striped.

# Haibara

1-9 Nihonbashi 2-chome Chuo-ku.      Tel. 272-3801.
**Hours:** 9: 00–5: 30 (Closed Sun. and Hols.).      Founded 1806.
**Specialty:** stationery and hand-made paper (*washi*).
Owner: Masao Nakamura (plus 20 employees).

Hand-made and hand-dyed papers, papers printed by wood-block, soft and rough textured papers—the variety will amaze you as you leaf through the sample catalogs of *washi* at the back counter of HAIBARA. Look also at the paper panels which come in sets of four and are used on the sliding doors called *fusuma*. These panels fit together to form a mural with the effect of a Japanese screen.

The first Nakamura-san of HAIBARA specialized in *gampi*, a soft, smooth white paper excellent for the calligraphic art of *waka* and *haiku* poems. Nakamura-san is also credited with designing the flat, circular summer fan (*uchiwa*) which became very popular in old Edo and is still in common use today.

The paper sold at HAIBARA today is made in the mountain villages of Kochi, Gifu and Fukui Prefectures by a 13-century-old process. Tree bark is dipped in water and wood ash and then soaked in a running stream or large basin for 48 hours. The cleaned bark is beaten into a pulp and mixed with a starch. A screen frame placed in the mixture is moved in all directions by hand. The pulp fibers become interwoven and form sheets of paper which are peeled off the screen.

**Shopping Hints:**           **Price range: ¥10–¥40,000**
—*Gampi* costs ¥150 for a 60 × 90 cm. sheet (2 × 3 feet). Tie-dyed paper (*chiyogami*) is priced from ¥100 to ¥400. White translucent paper used to protect gifts, sometimes mistakenly called rice paper, is called *kyo-hana oridashi* and is ¥450 a package.
—Gift items include: miniature folding screens called *byobu* (these are copies of antique treasures), origami paper mobiles, miniature sets of fans, summer *uchiwa*, and a folding paper lunch-box called *zansa-bukuro*. (This is an elegant doggy-bag for leftovers from a tea ceremony or restaurant meal.)

# Kammo

1-14 Muromachi 1-chome Nihonbashi Chuo-ku. Tel. 241-5417.
**Hours:** 9: 00–6: 00 (Closed Sun. & Hols.).    Founded 1673.
**Specialty:** fish paste products (*hampen*).
Owner: Mikio Inoue (plus mother, wife and 40 employees).

The cheerful, modern building with its tidy shop on the
ground floor and family living quarters above seems
an unlikely spot for the processing of huge chunks of
shark meat—but there in the back of the shop you can see
the fish being cut, ground, mixed with a starch paste,
pressed into shape and finally boiled in enormous kettles,
with the grandmother of the house busily turning each
white fish cake with a flat bamboo spoon or giant pair of
chopsticks.

KAMMO has been at its present location for 300 years,
and the family, whose members all participate in the
business, note with pride that their shop is prominently
listed in a record of famous Tokyo shops of the early
Meiji Period. Each day KAMMO produces 2,000 pieces of
their specialty *hampen*, as well as a golden deep-fried
fish-paste product called *agemono*.

*Hampen* is a soft white or pink cake that comes in both
square and oval forms. The oval-shaped cake is called
*hangetsu* or half-moon. *Hampen* is eaten fresh or grilled as
an anytime snack, often with sake. Along with *kamaboko*,
another popular and traditional fish-paste product, it is
usually included in ceremonial meals marking auspicious
occasions.

**Shopping Hints:**    **Price range: ¥20–¥2,500**
—One square or half-moon *hampen* is ¥100. A package of
  *kamaboko* costs from ¥450 to ¥650.
—*Agemono*, priced at ¥20 to ¥80 apiece, contain bits of
  shrimp, carrots, cheese, sesame seeds, vegetables or egg. Look
  at the wax model for a standard assortment for *oden*; ask for
  *oden dane*, and state how many people you wish to serve. The
  price is between ¥800 and ¥2,500.
—For something exotic to go with *hampen*, take home some
  *niko-gori*, a rich, dark bar of shark gelatin to be served in
  small slices as an hors d'oeuvre.

# Misucho

7 Kyobashi 1-chome Chuo-ku.     Tel. 561-0945.
**Hours:** 8 : 00–10 : 00 (Open every day).     Founded 1773.
**Specialty:** bamboo shades (*sudare, misu*).
Owner: Taichi Kamiyama (plus wife, son and daughter).

A shop so tiny that the customer can hardly enter, MISUCHO is located in a section of Nihonbashi that once housed many artisans. Each block of the area was devoted to the production of a single product—thus Ogacho was Big Saw Town.

The owner of MISUCHO, Kamiyama-san, loves to tell how his father, when only 10 years old, tried to buy a weaving device for shades which he had seen at a fair. Kamiyama-san, now in his 80's, concedes that he inherited his father's zeal and that his skill and hard work have made him the "king" of bamboo shade makers. One of his shades hanges in the Imperial Palace, and many of his innovations have become standard techniques of the craft.

The traditional shade for decorative purposes or room separation is the *sudare*. Thin reeds, rather than bamboo, are used in special *sudare* for tea houses. *Misu*, the shade used in shrines, can be distinguished from *sudare* by four strands of silk binding and two elaborate tassels. (All the tassels are made by Mrs. Kamiyama.) The twisted rope curtain seen at the entrance to tea houses and traditional bars is called *nawa noren*.

The most difficult part of shade-making is to match the slightly uneven strips of bamboo so that the finished shade hangs perfectly straight. Kamiyama-san says this is a skill requiring 10 years to master.

**Shopping Hints:**          **Price range: ¥1,500–¥68,000**
—*Sudare* cost from ¥1,500 to ¥29,000 depending upon the type of bamboo and the quality of the string. (Eight types of bamboo or reed are available.) The standard size is 3 × 4 ft.
—*Misu*, 3-feet wide, cost up to ¥68,000.
—Hand-made brooms, *hōki*, cost ¥1,200 for the traditional short-handled kind and ¥1,900 for a long-handled one.

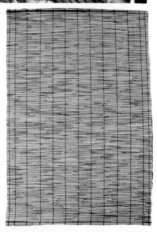

# Token Shibata
Map (p. 73, Nihonbashi #6)

2 Nihonbashi Honcho 4-chome Chuo-ku.    Tel. 661-0088.
**Hours:** 9: 00–5: 00 (Closed Sun. and Hols.).    Founded 1913.
**Specialty:** swords and armor (*katana* and *yoroi*).
Owner: Mitsuo Shibata (plus 25 employees).

The wide store-front of TOKEN SHIBATA is in the style of an old Japanese storehouse. Shibata-san's father, who founded the shop, traded no more than 3 or 4 swords a month to a few carefully selected customers. Today the son whose business is bustling and profitable still reveres his father's "superior," disinterested love for swords.

Experts divide Japanese swords into 4 historical groups: *kotoh*, from the 9th to the 17th century; *shintoh*, from the 17th century to 1830; *shin-shintoh*, from 1830 to the Meiji Restoration; and *gendai*, from Meiji to the present. During the *kotoh* period, changing battle tactics influenced the design of swords. The development of cavalry required longer swords and, to pierce the armor of Mongolian forces, the points were later tapered and made sharper. With the introduction of guns in the 16th century the importance of infantry increased, and swords became shorter. Also, the sword's carrying position was reversed so that the sharp edge faced upwards, allowing for a faster draw in hand-to-hand combat. With the rise of the *samurai* class a cult of the sword developed. The sword was not only a weapon, but also the warrior's badge of honor—it was thought to be his very soul.

**Shopping Hints:**        **Price range: ¥20,000–¥20,000,000**
—From the earliest *kotoh* period, extremely complicated tempering techniques produced layers of steel which are visible and are considered a mark of beauty. In Tokugawa times patterns of waves or flames were produced. Antique swords cost from ¥500,000 to ¥20,000,000.
—*Tsuba*, or sword-guards, are collectors' pieces in themselves; so are *menuki*, metal ornaments of birds, flowers or gods. They cost ¥20,000 to ¥1,000,000.
—An average price for a suit of armor in the *gusoku* style (small metal pieces tied with silk cord) is ¥1,200,000.

## Tsurukawa Gakki-ten Map (p. 73, Nihonbashi #7)

1-4 Takara-cho Chuo-ku.       Tel. 561-1872.
**Hours:** 9: 00–6: 00 (Open every day).       Founded 1793.
**Specialty:** Japanese harps (*koto*).
Owner: Fujio Tsurukawa (plus 6 employees).

Seven generations ago the founder of this shop, Tsuru-kawa Tango-no-Kami, was a *koto* craftsman in the service of the feudal lord of Date. Tsurukawa-san lived in the Takara-cho district of Tokyo where many other crafts-men patronized by wealthy families also worked. *Samurai*, arriving by palanquins to order a *koto* from Tsurukawa-san or to browse through the antiques available on Nakadori street, were once familiar sights in the area that is still known for its fine shops.

The *koto*, a 13-stringed instrument, came to Japan from China in the 8th century. Two schools of playing developed: *Ikutaryu* in Kyoto where the *koto* was used harmonically with the *shamisen*, and *Yamadaryu* in Tokyo where the *koto* played the melody. About 50 years ago Michio Miyagi, a master of the *Ikuta* school, developed with the owner of this shop a special 17-stringed *koto* whose music is called *shin nihon ongaku*. Students often play Italian baroque music with this new *koto*.

The *koto* is made of light weight paulownia wood, *kiri*. Wood cut farthest from the core is the hardest and therefore the best. The grain, too, is important not only for esthetic reasons but also for its effect on the sound which follows the grain and should flow evenly off both sides and out through the holes at the back. The wood is sun-dried and then stays in the shade for several years. A single craftsman works on the *koto* from the time the wood is selected until the instrument is finished. He cuts the wood, fits it together, burns and polishes the surface, fin-ishes the ends and attaches the strings. A correctly tuned *koto* has $2\frac{1}{2}$ octaves. The pick is of ivory or plastic.

**Shopping Hints:**       **Price range: ¥70,000–¥1,000,000**
—A practice *koto* may be purchased for ¥70,000. Professional instruments begin at ¥200,000 and go as high as ¥1,000,000.

# Yagicho

4 Muro-machi 1-chome Nihonbashi Chuo-ku.       Tel. 241-1211.
**Hours:** 9: 00–6: 00 (Open every day).       Founded 1743.
**Specialty:** dried bonito fish (*katsuobushi*).
Owner: Chobei Yagi (plus 13 employees).

YAGICHO, established in the old *katsuobushi* whole-
sale district at the edge of the original Nihonbashi fish
market, prospered for three generations but then endured
a period of decline until the present owner's grandfather
revitalized it. The present owner, displaying the true
independent *Edokko* spirit, recently refused to sell his
corner lot to the bank next door, and the bank was forced
to build its large modern structure around the little shop.

The chunks of dried bonito lining one wall of YAGICHO
look for all the world like useless bits of driftwood. They
are, however, essential to Japanese cooking, for in flaked
form the fish is used in the stock basic to all soups and
many vegetable and fish dishes. To make *katsuobushi*,
fresh bonito is cut into fillets, boiled, smoked and sun-
dried for as long as 3 months. The dried fish is shaved into
thin peelings (best done fresh each day) for use in cooking.
Fish caught in May and processed in Kagoshima and
Kochi Prefectures are the most highly prized.

In the past, wealthy families used *katsuobushi* as a
bartering item, and *samurai* carried dried chunks of bonito
along with their swords to the battlefield. Its high cost
prevented rural families from enjoying it till after World
War II, and stories were told of its being the most frequently dreamed of food among countryside folk.

**Shopping Hints:**                    **Price range: ¥330–¥13,000**
—*Katsuobushi* ranges in price from ¥330 for one piece to
¥13,000 for an austere but elegant gift box.
—Large flakes of *katsuobushi* are ¥250 for 100 grams ($3\frac{1}{2}$ oz.).
Less flavorsome fine shavings are ¥180.
—Dried mushrooms, many kinds of beans and various Chinese
dried foods are also available.
—Note the wet little towels near the door. Customers may use
them after making their selection.

# Kashiwa-ya

3-13 Shintomi-cho 3-chome Chuo-ku.     Tel. 551-1362.
**Hours:** 8: 00–10: 00 (Open every day).     Founded 1848.
**Specialty:** paper lanterns (*chochin*).
Owner: Saburo Ueno (plus mother and wife).

Four generations ago the founder of KASHIWA-YA was a skilled letterer of signboards for *kabuki* dramas. The second generation designed and cut the intricate paper patterns used in stencil-dyed cloth. Today the Ueno family puts the finishing touches on lanterns made in Gifu and Ibaraki Prefectures. After painting the background color, they add either a family crest or the name of a shop. The *sumi* ink used for this design must be stirred for an hour to produce a single cupful of the desired thickness.

Paper lanterns, *chochin*, were originally used at religious services. The folding variety that we know today developed in the late 1500's. During the Tokugawa Period, *chochin* came into common use, and different varieties were designated for firemen, merchants, detectives and craftsmen. Today *chochin* decorate religious and festival sites, the *kabuki* stage and restaurants. Small bars (*nomi-ya*) and neighborhood restaurants selling *oden* or *sushi* place large, round, red lanterns outside their shops; more expensive restaurants often have their elegant emblem or name written on a long, tan lantern.

The largest lantern made by Ueno-san, measuring 6 × 8 feet, now hangs in front of the *Kabuki-za* Theater in the Ginza.

**Shopping Hints:**                **Price range: ¥800–¥50,000**
—The lanterns decorating the *Kabuki-za* Theater are made by the Ueno family (and replaced by them every three months). You may order a similar lantern for ¥5,000. A miniature souvenir *Kabuki-za* lantern costs ¥800.
—A traditional lantern meant to be carried while on horseback is called *bajo chochin* and has a long flexible handle to be tucked into the rider's sash. Ueno-san makes them to order.
—A cylindrical lantern with a handle and a hook for hanging is ¥3,000. Called *yumihari chochin*, it usually has the shop or family name written in black ink on the natural paper.

# Kuno-ya

9-8 Ginza 6-chome Chuo-ku.　　Tel. 571-2546.
**Hours:** 10:00–8:00 (Closed 3rd Mon.).　　Founded 1837.
**Specialty:** kimono accessories (*waso-komono*).
Owner: Yasaburo Kikuchi (plus 20 employees).

The imaginative and high-quality kimono accessories at KUNO-YA will delight the foreign shopper, for many items can be used beautifully with western clothes. This stylish shop began six generations ago when the founder, Kikuchi-san, began to make and sell hemp products. The shop's cords and nets, used for fishing and duck hunting in the nearby swamps of what is now the Ginza, became well-known. Much later, the time-honored shop was commissioned by Meiji officials to provide cotton cords for the conductor poles on top of Tokyo's newly inaugurated streetcars.

In 1922 the present shop opened, selling primarily *obijime*, the decorative cords worn over the *obi* sash. Occasionally the craftsmen at KUNO-YA would use cords like *obijime* as the strings on traditional handbags, and the shop became known for its imaginatively styled purses. Handbags, called *fukuromono*, began to be produced regularly after the war, with the present owner continuing to experiment with new fabrics and designs. Kimono undergarments were also added to the shop's merchandise. An elaborate array of slips, sashes and other garments must be put on and tied before milady is ready to slip into the outer kimono and *obi*.

**Shopping Hints:**　　　　　**Price range: ¥200–¥150,000**

—Handbags of cotton, silk and wax-dyed leather come in many shapes. From ¥3,000 to more than ¥40,000.
—A 7-colored silk *kimono* cord, *objime*, is the pride of this shop. It is made from the 5 Imperial Court colors plus gold and silver, and can be adapted to western styles. Price ¥2,000.
—*Obiage*, wide sashes worn tucked into the *obi*, are often tie-dyed in delicate patterns; about ¥5,000. (For little girls similar sashes function as summer kimono *obi*.)
—*Obi-makura*, literally sash-pillow, is the pad used under the back bow of the *obi* to hold it in place. ¥850.

# Kyu-kyo-do

7-4 Ginza 5-chome Chuo-ku.　　Tel. 571-4429.
**Hours:** 10: 00–7: 30 (Closed Sun.).　　Founded 1663.
**Specialty:** incense (*koh*).
Owner: Naomichi Kumagai (plus 56 employees).

*Koh*, incense, was brought to Japan by a Chinese Buddhist priest in 754 and gradually became popular with the nobility. Competing with each other to produce pleasing new scents, court families developed a cere-monial cult called *kohdo* which is still practiced today.

The Kumagai family of KYU-KYO-DO traces its line-age back almost 800 years to the Genji family. The shop, established in Kyoto in 1663, dealt in herbs and incense, the latter used in certain medical cures. Gradually the varieties of incense carried by the shop increased, and by the 6th generation it was providing incense for the Imperial Family and members of the court. After the Meiji restoration the Tokyo shop was opened and was granted approval by the Imperial Family to make and sell six secret mixed incenses which, for almost a thousand years, had been used exclusively by the Emperor's Family and court.

**Shopping Hints:**　　　　**Price range: ¥250–¥500,000**

—There are three different forms of incense: *kohboku*, chips of wood from 10 naturally scented trees, often used in the tea and *kohdo* ceremonies, smokeless (¥250–¥1,500); *neriko*, a small black cone combining the powdered woods of several different trees, invented by the Japanese 900 years ago, also smokeless (¥400–¥1,800); *senkoh*, a stick of incense which produces smoke as well as scent, used exclusively in religious rituals and offerings for the dead (¥150–¥30,000).

—*Mukusa no takimono*, the secret scents of the Imperial Family, may be purchased separately in attractive containers. *Kuro-bou* is used all year round. The others are used seasonally, as suggested by their names: *kayou* (lotus leaf), *baika* (plum blossom), *kikuka* (chrysanthemum), *jijyu* (Imperial cham-berlain) and *ochiba* (fallen leaves). ¥4,000 each.

—Tiles and stands for incense burning, brocade sachets, prayer heads and other gift items are also available.

# Masuda-ya

8-15 Ginza 2-chome Chuo-ku.    Tel. 561-3362.
**Hours:** 12: 00–7: 00 (Closed Sun. and Hols.).    Founded 1923.
**Specialty:** kimono, *haori* and *obi* cloth; also dyeing (*gofuku*).
Owner: Yoshio Umeda (plus wife and sister).

Corners cluttered with old canes, a princely doll and other attic treasures, a tasteful display of folk craft and family antiques—these bits of old Japan provide a charming backdrop for the exquisite silks that you can choose for kimono, *haori* jackets and *obi* sashes.

The father of MASUDA-YA's present owner was originally a wholesaler of cotton cloth. His wife, from a Tokyo family of dyers, helped his customers choose patterns and colors for their material. And so there developed a special service which the shop continues to offer today: it will have skilled dyers prepare fabric to the customer's specifications. (One of MASUDA-YA's dyers is a Living National Treasure.) Do look at the pattern and color catalogs containing a fantastic range of rainbow hues.

One special fabric available at the shop is *komon*. A Tokyo-developed fabric, *komon* was used during Tokugawa days for the garments of *samurai* and later became popular with women. An intricate stencil made from several layers of paper is used to make a subtle pattern of dots and fine lines. Not particularly striking from a distance, *komon* reveals a delicate beauty upon close inspection.

**Shopping Hints:**    **Price range: ¥5,000–¥1,200,000**
—Some fabrics are intended only for a particular type of occasion; the appropriateness of others is determined by the wearer's age. At MASUDA-YA silks are available up to ¥1,200,000 (the price of an elegant wedding kimono).
—*Komon* costs between ¥45,000 and ¥100,000.
—Summer kimono are called *yukata*. Perhaps the most useful item for foreigners, the prices of *yukata* fabric are low (from ¥5,000 for 12 meters) and the designs lovely. The *yukata*, which MASUDA-YA will have sewn for you, can be worn as a robe or loungewear, and is the proper dress for the *bon-odori* community dances during July and August.

# Ohno-ya-sohon-ten

2 Shintomi-cho 2-chome Chuo-ku.  Tel. 551-0896.
**Hours:** 10: 00–8: 00 (Closed Sun.).  Founded 1772.
**Specialty:** traditional socks (*tabi*).
Owner: Yasuo Fukushima (plus 30 employees).

OHNO-YA, a pleasant corner shop, has for six generations made and sold *tabi*, the single-toed socks worn with
kimono. Originally the shop sold men's undergarments;
but when the founder moved his shop close to the old
Shintomi-za Theater, *kabuki* actors began to ask him to
make their *tabi*. *Kabuki* actors, who wear out 50 pairs
of *tabi* a month, continue to be OHNO-YA's best customers. Another famous customer was the late Prime
Minister Yoshida who loved to wear traditional dress; *tabi*
became a symbol of his term of office.

Originally *tabi* was an outdoor leather shoe, but during
the Tokugawa Era indoor *tabi* of cotton and sometimes
silk became popular. By Meiji times only geisha continued
to go barefoot with formal kimono. Early *tabi* opened
at the front and were fastened by strings, but during
the Edo Period metal clasps at the side were used. The
clasps continue to be popular today. Formerly, *tabi* were
loose fitting, but today they should cling tightly to foot
and ankle.

At OHNO-YA more than 400 pairs of *tabi* a day are
made in the second-floor workshop. Stitching the single,
rounded toe is the most difficult part of the work, requiring
an unusual sewing machine and special training.

**Shopping Hints:**  Price range: ¥550–¥7,000
—White, colored or printed *tabi* come in 4 widths: *botan*
  (peony) is very wide with a high instep; *ume* (plum blossom) is
  wide; *yanagi* (willow) is medium; and *hoso* means narrow.
  ¥950 a pair.
—Special silk *tabi* worn to weddings cost ¥1,500 a pair.
—*Tenugui*, small cloths used in Japanese dances and in other
  towel-like ways, are made to order and printed with special
  designs or crests often related to *kabuki* dramas or actors.
—You will also find cloth purses (¥550), kimono jackets
  (¥2,000 to ¥7,000) and little telephone pillows (¥1,200).

# Ryuzen-do

Map (p. 91, Ginza-Tsukiji #7)

8-6 Ginza 5-chome Chuo-ku.     Tel. 571-4321.
**Hours:** 10: 00–8: 00 (Closed 3rd Sun.).     Founded 1883.
**Specialty:** tea ceremony utensils (*cha-dogu*).
Owner: Ikuko Nagata (plus 2 employees).

A modest little shop, RYUZEN-DO carries more than 500 items related to that most venerable of Japanese arts, the tea ceremony.

The first known use of powdered green tea in Japan goes back to the 13th century when Zen Buddhist monks developed ceremonial drinking cults within their temple compounds. By the 16th century tea drinking had become a pleasurable pastime of the upper classes who used expensive tea bowls inspired by Chinese designs, colors and techniques. At the end of the 16th century the appearance of three tea masters brought great changes in tea-drinking practices. One man in particular, Sen no Rikyu, taught his followers to appreciate the beauty and simplicity of everyday Japanese and Korean pottery.

Within the Sen family (descendants of Sen no Rikyu) three major schools of tea ceremony originated. The family in turn employed talented craftsmen and their families to provide the utensils for the new tea-drinking practices. These families, still living in Kyoto in their 9th to 15th generations, have been producing tea ceremony utensils for over 300 years. Items made by these craftsmen are available at RYUZEN-DO.

**Shopping Hints:**                    Price range: ¥50–¥3,000,000
—There are 5 general kinds of tea ceremony utensils: vases and scrolls, etc., to decorate the room; tea bowls, canisters, whisks and scoops for making and serving tea; lacquered trays, rice bowls, etc., for serving the meal; straw mats, gong, etc., for placement outside the tea room; charcoal basket, water jar, etc., for the washing and preparation area.
—Tea bowls cost from ¥1,000 to ¥500,000 depending on the maker, age and style. Lacquered plates in 4 sizes are priced at ¥3,500 to ¥8,000. Vases begin at ¥3,000.
—A form of tea ceremony called *Sencha* uses tiny cups and a teapot. From ¥6,000 to ¥25,000.

105

# Tsumugi-ya
Map (p. 91, Ginza-Tsukiji #8)

9-20 Ginza 5-chome Chuo-ku.    Tel. 571-0993.
**Hours:** 10: 00–7: 00 (Closed Sun.).    Founded 1813.
**Specialty:** hand-spun silk (*tsumugi*).
Owner: Tsukiko Urasawa (plus 8 employees).

The history of TSUMUGI-YA begins across the island in Niigata Prefecture where for three generations the firm was a wholesaler of a famous local linen crepe (*echigo-jofu*). Then Tokyo beckoned, the founder's grandson brought his cloth to the capital and peddled it from a hand-drawn cart till he had earned enough to open a shop.

Of the 4 kinds of traditional hand-spun cloth and the 2 varieties which the shop developed itself, *yuki-tsumugi* has the most fascinating history. During the Edo Period, the rising merchant class was forbidden by government decree to live ostentatiously. Paying lip-service to the law, wealthy merchants often turned to *yuki-tsumugi* as a way of satisfying their taste for the elegant; for, although at first glance the fabric seems plain and cheap, it is in reality extremely costly. The painstaking efforts required in its manufacture make the high cost understandable. Two or three months are needed to spin the silk threads, another three months are spent just marking the threads for dyeing with colors taken from wild grasses, and 6 months are required to weave the fabric. One year's work to make the material for one kimono! But what makes the cloth famous is not simply the time and effort it requires but its natural dye coloring which actually becomes brighter with age. It is said that a kimono made from *yuki-tsumugi* may be worn for more than 100 years.

**Shopping Hints:**        **Price range: ¥49,000–¥2,000,000**
—A length of *yuki-tsumugi*, 35 cm. by 12 m. (13½ inches × 40 feet), costs from ¥180,000 to ¥2,000,000.
—The two hand-spun fabrics developed by the shop are *koten-tsumugi* and *bandai-tsumugi*. From ¥60,000 to ¥100,000.
—*Echigo-jofu*, bleached by ultra-violet rays reflected against deep snow in Niigata Prefecture, costs from ¥150,000 to ¥700,000.

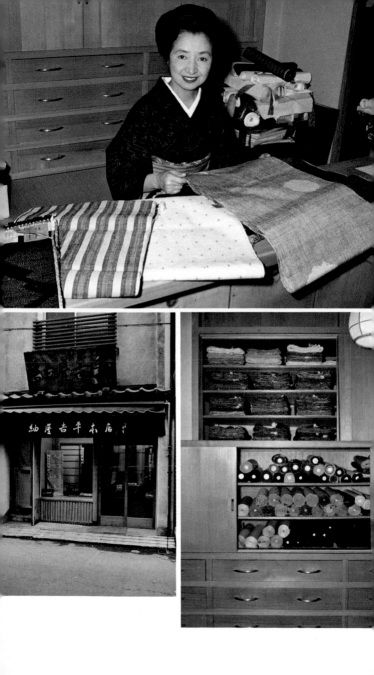

# OTHER AREAS
## TORANOMON AND SHIBA

On the moat surrounding Edo Castle (now the Imperial Palace) there was once a gate called Torano-gomon, and from this gate the district took its name. Many *samurai* lived in the streets south of the gate, and the area was dotted with temples. The largest temple, Zohjoh-ji in Shiba Park, was the official temple of the Tokugawa family. Today, the elegant antique shops and galleries that line the main street from Toranomon to Tokyo Tower in Shiba Park are reminders of the days when wealthy *samurai* with luxurious tastes rambled through the neighborhood.

## HONGO

The rich student life of Hongo District is immortalized in many classic Meiji novels. Little remains of this Bohemian atmosphere today; but when you stroll past Tokyo University you will see one of its landmarks—the Akamon, or Red Gate, near the main entrance to the campus. The Akamon, which has been designated a National Treasure, dates back to the Edo Period when the property belonged to the wealthy Maeda family.

## WAKAMATSUCHO

The streets around Shinjuku Station are filled with bars, coffee houses, restaurants, neon signs and an air of perpetual excitement. In Edo times, it was a small town where people spent the last night of their journey from Koshu, west of Tokyo. One mile northeast of Shinjuku Station is a small area called Wakamatsucho where you will find Bingoya, the folkcraft shop described below.

1. **Bingo-ya** 備後屋（河田町バス停前）⇨pp.110 & 111.
2. **Aoki Uemon Shoten** 青木宇右衛門商店（東大農学部前の道を斜めに入り左側）⇨pp.112 & 113.
3. **Maezawa Goban-ten** 前沢碁盤店（壱岐坂、本富士派出所西隣） ⇨pp.114 & 115.
4. **Ishida Biwa-ten** 石田琵琶店（虎の門交差点より東京タワー方向に向い2つ目の信号を左に曲る）⇨pp.116 & 117.
5. **Nagasawa In-ten** 長沢印店（地下鉄銀座線虎の門駅近く） ⇨pp.118 & 119.

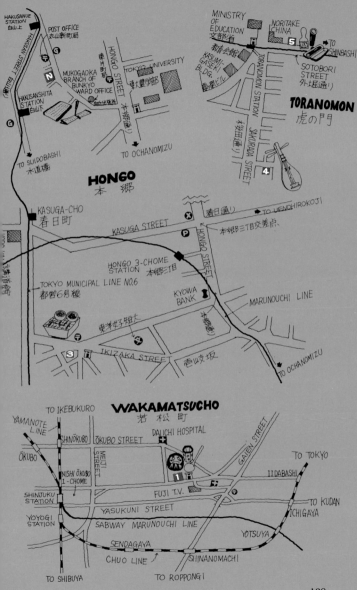

# Bingo-ya

Map (p. 109, Others #1)

69 Wakamatsu-cho Shinjuku-ku.    Tel. 202-8778.
**Hours:** 10:00–7:00 (Closed Mon.).    Founded 1948.
**Specialty:** folkcrafts (*mingeihin*).
Owner: Hiromu Okada (6 family members and 10 employees).

Folkcraft was far from Okada-san's mind when he opened his Tokyo shop. His family in Hiroshima were *tatami* wholesalers, and he was to provide a Tokyo outlet for their wares. However, influenced by his younger brother, an artist, he began to stock baskets hand-woven in the Hiroshima countryside. Housewives found the baskets useful for shopping, and Okada-san was encouraged by their approval to sell more and more folkcraft articles. Gradually, *tatami* floor mats were abandoned altogether. Today BINGOYA, an attractive building designed to resemble a traditional storehouse, contains six floors brimming with folk toys, baskets, pottery, hand-dyed fabrics, lacquerware and country furniture.

The word *mingei* means something like "crafts of the masses"; but today due to the folkcraft boom *mingei* often means little more than "souvenirs"—the sort of trinkets one finds in train stations. BINGOYA sells none of these souvenirs. Its items carry all the earmarks of true *mingei*: they are practical things, made simply and strongly for everyday use; they are usually unsigned by the maker; and they originate in local customs and reflect the unique color and flavor of their region. *Ko-mingei* are articles no longer produced or used today—the antiques of folkcraft; *shin-mingei* are still being produced and used today in the villages and towns of Japan.

**Shopping Hints:**    **Price range: ￥30–￥300,000**
Set of lacquerware soup bowls are priced at ￥1,500–￥13,000. Hand-dyed cloth begins at ￥1,500. Temple charms and good-luck toys may be bought for less than ￥500. Wooden plates begin at ￥200. About 10 kinds of traditional *kokeshi* dolls come from 6 northern prefectures; from ￥500 to ￥6,000. And there are drums, masks, kites, countryside straw raincoats, tea bowls, vases and boxes made from the bark of cherry trees.

# Aoki Uemon-shoten

Map (p. 109, Others #2)

16-25 Nishikata-machi 2-chome Bunkyo-ku.      Tel. 811-0738.
**Hours:** 8:00–4:00 (Closed Sun. and 1st & 15th of the month).
**Specialty:** straw mats (*tatami*).      Founded 1773.
Owner: Uemon Aoki (plus 5 employees).


As early as the 6th century *tatami* floor mats were placed over a raised area at one corner of the room and used as a bed. In the 11th century raised *tatami* areas became seats for honored guests, and in the 13th century rooms began to be completely covered with *tatami*.

Today *tatami* are made in 2 sizes. Tokyo-style is 6 × 3 feet, and Kyoto-Osaka style is 5 inches longer and $2\frac{1}{2}$ inches wider. The mats are made from 2-inch thick mattresses of rough straw padding which is covered with a thin mat of *igusa* rush. The finely woven rush mat is stitched by hand to the straw mattress and then is finished with binding. Usually the binding is a plain color—maroon being the most popular—but sometimes binding with elaborate patterns and gold or silver threads are used. Aoki-san and his employees can hand-stitch the bindings on to 6 mats a day; if they use a special sewing machine, they can finish 12.

*Tatami* are set into an indented floor. Nothing is used to hold them in place, but because all traditional rooms are measured by the number of mats they will hold, the fit is extraordinarily precise.

Aoki-san's family history goes back to the 14th century Kamakura Period when the family owned large areas of land in the district now called Hongo. The 19th generation of the family began to make and sell *tatami* to the families of Edo. Today Aoki-san personally visits homes to check on the condition of the mats a year after installation.

**Shopping Hints:**              **Price range: ¥5,000–¥20,000**
—New mats cost ¥5,000 to ¥20,000 and should last for 20 years. For an additional 3-years' wear, the rush surface mat can be changed or simply turned over, and new binding sewn on. Turning over the rush mat costs ¥1,500 to ¥5,000.

# Maezawa-goban-ten

18-6 Hongo 1-chome Bunkyo-ku.      Tel. 812-3331.
**Hours:** 8:00–8:00 (Closed Sun.).      Founded 1890.
**Specialty:** *go* boards and stones (*goban* and *goishi*).
Owner: Setsuko Maezawa (plus 2 sons and 5 craftsmen).

Early in the Meiji Period, the Maezawa family began to sell the sets of black and white stones used in the game of *go*. Soon they were making and selling *go*-boards as well as the stones. Today, the two great-grandsons of the shop's founder still go into the mountains to choose and help cut the trees. Wood from the *kaya* (torrey pine) is the best. To be large enough for a 6-inch thick *go*-board, the tree must be an incredible 700 to 800 years old. After drying for 15 years, the wood is polished with natural wax and the intersecting playing lines are painted on. Master players say the *go*-board takes on various expressions depending on the thickness of the black lacquered lines.

The 4 short legs resemble a gardenia seed, which leads to a Japanese pun. *Kuchi-nashi* means not only "gardenia," but also "don't be a kibitzer." It is alleged that the shallow hole on the underside of the board, is put there to receive the blood of the kibitzer who should be beheaded for disturbing the game. In reality, its function is to increase the sharp click of the stones as they are placed in play.

MAEZAWA-GOBAN-TEN also makes *shogi* (Japanese chess) sets. The wooden chess pieces, or *koma*, are lettered with Chinese characters which determine their value in the game. Only 2 craftsmen in all Tokyo know how to paint the thick lacquered characters on the *koma*.

**Shopping Hints:**          **Price range: ¥2,000–¥2,000,000**
—*Go*-boards of *kaya* cost ¥100,000 to ¥2,000,000. Cheaper boards are made of *katsura* (Judas tree). A 3-inch *katsura* board is ¥20,000 and a 6-inch board is ¥65,000.
—*Go* uses 180 white stones cut from clam shells and 181 black stones cut from natural rock. These sets cost from ¥7,000 to ¥500,000. Glass stones cost only ¥2,000 and ¥3,000.
—*Shogi*-boards are usually half the price of *go*-boards. The *koma* pieces cost between ¥10,000 and ¥80,000.

# Ishida-biwa-ten

Map (p. 109, Others #4)

89 Shiba Nishikubo Tomoe-cho Minato-ku.    Tel. 431-6548.
**Hours:** 8: 30–10: 00 (Open every day).    Founded 1878.
**Specialty:** Japanese lute (*biwa*).    Owner: Fushiki Ishida.

The *biwa*, a lute-like instrument, came to Japan from China in the 8th century. In the 16th century, the feudal lord of Satsuma (Kagoshima Prefecture) asked a priest to compose an inspirational song on his *biwa* for the *samurai* of the district. The fame of this song spread as far as Edo, and the type of *biwa* on which it was written became very popular. There are several types of *biwa* available today, but the *satsuma-biwa* is still the most popular.

Mulberry is the best wood for *biwa*. Cheaper instruments are made of zelkova wood whose natural light color becomes dark and lustrous with use. Ishida-san, the 4th generation owner of the shop, looks for wood with parallel grains, for this kind of grain produces a clear tone.

The *biwa* has two sections—the body and the lid which includes the angular neck. Two tiny openings with moon-shaped decorations and a larger opening under the base of the strings are essential for the tone. Two decorative strips of whalebone are inserted across the widest part, and bridges of wood and ivory are placed on the neck. Four silk strings of graduated thickness are then tied in place.

It takes Ishida-san 10 days to make one biwa. Each has a unique tone, and as he begins to work on a new one, he will frequently tap the wood and take pleasure in anticipating the sound that this new instrument will have.

The patron-deity of music is Benten-san who is always represented as a beautiful woman holding a *biwa*. In former days, many court musicians remained single lest Benten-san become jealous and take away their talent.

**Shopping Hints:**              **Price range: ¥100,000–¥300,000**
—*Biwa* made from zelkova wood start at ¥100,000. Mulberry-wood *biwa* for professional use start at ¥250,000.
—Plectrums of camellia wood cost ¥9,000. Better quality boxwood plectrums are ¥40,000.

# Nagasawa In-ten

Map (p. 109, Others #5)

27 Shiba-Toranomon Minato-ku.    Tel. 591-7381.
**Hours:** 9: 00–6: 00 (Closed Sun. and Hols.).    Founded 1831.
**Specialty:** family and business seals (*han* or *hanko*).
Owner: Yorihiro Nagasawa (plus 20 employees).


During the Nara Period, *hanko* seals were used on government documents, and in Edo times they became popular among nobles and the middle classes. Today a written signature is almost never used in Japan, for the Meiji government ruled that everyone must use registered *hanko* on business contracts and legal documents.

The registered *hanko* bears the name of the family or company written in Chinese characters. Usually carved in ivory or stone, it is used for only the most important documents. A cheaper wooden seal, not registered, is carried in one's pocket for daily use. Artists and calligraphers use a larger, decorative *hanko* to stamp their works. Carvers of *hanko* often pass a government examination which awards 2 ranks depending upon the craftsman's skill.

The present owner of NAGASAWA IN-TEN explains that when he designs a *hanko*, he tries to embody in his design the meaning of the name. A record of originally designed seals is kept in a series of albums dating back to the origins of the shop. In these albums you can see the *hanko* of many famous men, including that of the present Prime Minister, Kakuei Tanaka.


**Shopping Hints:**              **Price range: ¥2,000–¥2,000,000**
—Seals are made from ivory, crystal, marble, bone, soapstone, semi-precious stones and various kinds of wood. A medium-priced wood seal with your name in Chinese characters can be ordered for ¥2,000. A red ink-pad, called *shu-niku*, costs ¥1,000 to ¥25,000.
—Companies require 3 or more seals: *sha-in*, the company's name seal; *war-in*, a revenue stamp; *Yaku-shoku-in*, the names of the company exectuives. From ¥40,000 to ¥700,000.
—Calling cards, *meishi*, with your name in both Japanese and English, cost ¥2,500 for 100.

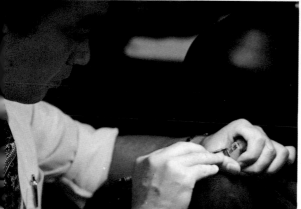

# How to "Read" Japanese

The Japanese names in this guide are given in Romanized writing. It will be helpful in your shopping if you practice the pronunciation in advance.

A..."ah" as in father, alms (not **a** as in at or ate).

E..."eh" as in enter, feather, met (not **e** as in beet).

I..."ee" as in eat, she, meat (not **i** as in it).

O..."oh" as in open, go, so (not **o** as in pot).

U..."oo" as in pool, soup (not **u** as in up).

G...hard "G" as in get, girl, give (not **g** as in gem).

F ...You can read it as "F" or "H", the Japanese sound is half-way between.

## Japanese Phrases for Shopping

When nobody is in the shop front, call GOMEN KUDASAI (Hey there!).

What's the name of this shop?

> KONO MISENO NAMAE WA NAN DESKA?

Do you have this one?

> KORE WA ARIMASKA?

May I see the one in the window?

> WINDOH NO NAKA NO SORE O MISETE KUDASAI?

Please show me the black one.

> KUROI NO O MISETE KUDASAI.

| | | | |
|---|---|---|---|
| white | SHIROI | light | AKARUI |
| red | AKAI | dark | KURAI |
| blue | AOI or BURU | long | NAGAI |
| yellow | KIIROI | short | MIJIKAI |
| green | MIDORI or | big | OHKII |
| | GURIN | small | CHIISAI |
| brown | CHAIROI | expensive | TAKAI |
| pink | MOMOIRO or | inexpensive | YASUI |
| | PINKU | | |

Please show me some others.
> HOKANO O MISETE KUDASAI.

I'll take this one.
> KORE O KUDASAI.

May I try this on?
> KITEMITE MO II DESKA?

Can I order one?
> CHUMON DEKIMASKA?

How long will it take?
> NAN NICHI KAKARIMASKA?

When will it be ready?
> ITSU DEKI AGARIMASKA?

Please wrap it as a gift.
> OKURIMONO DESKARA TSUTSUNDE KUDASAI.

I'd like three of these.
> KORE MITTSU (or three) KUDASAI.

| one | HITOTSU | six | MUTTSU |
|-----|---------|------|----------|
| two | FUTATSU | seven | NANATSU |
| three | MITTSU | eight | YATTSU |
| four | YOTTSU | nine | KOKONOTSU |
| five | ITSUTSU | ten | TOH |

I don't understand.
> WAKARIMASEN.

Do you speak English?
> EIGO GA WAKARIMASKA?

Where is the public telephone?
> KOSHU DENWA WA DOKODESKA?

Please draw me a map.
> CHIZU O KAITE KUDASAI.

Where is the nearest station?
> ICHIBAN CHIKAI EKI WA DOKO DESKA?

Please call me a taxi for me.
> TAKUSHI O YONDE KUDASAI.

# CHRONOLOGY

## (Including the dates when the shops were founded)

| | |
|---|---|
| **—600 A.D.** | **FOUNDING OF THE COUNTRY** |
| | And the First Foreign Influence |
| 552 | Official introduction of Buddhism from Korea to the Japanese court. |
| **600—794** | **ASUKA AND NARA PERIOD** |
| | Period of Political Reforms, Growth of Buddhism |
| 604 | Seventeen-article "Constitution" |
| 630 | First Embassy to T'ang dynasty |
| 708 | First issuance of copper coinage |
| 752 | Dedication of Great Buddha of Nara |
| **794—1185** | **HEIAN PERIOD** |
| | Growth of a Native Culture |
| 838 | Twelfth and last embassy to T'ang |
| 889 | Granting of surname Taira (Heike) to great-grandson of Emperor Kammu and progenitor of warrior Taira family |
| 905 | Compilation of *Kokinshu* by Ki no Tsurayuki |
| 951 | Establishment of *Waka-dokoro* (Poetry Commission) |
| 961 | Granting of surname Minamoto (Genji) to grandson of Emperor Seiwa and progenitor of warrior Minamoto family |
| 1002 | Writing of *Makura no Soshi* (*Pillow Book*) by Lady Sei Shonagon |
| 1008–20 | Writing of *Genji Monogatari* (*Tale of Genji*) by Lady Murasaki |
| 1052–62 | Earlier Nine Years' War |
| 1083–7 | Later Three Years' War |
| 1180–5 | War between the Minamoto and Taira (Gempei Wars), destruction of Taira |

## 1185—1333 KAMAKURA PERIOD
### Development of a Feudal Society

| | |
|---|---|
| 1191 | Introduction of the Rinzai branch of the Zen sect from China |
| 1206 | Compilation of *Shinkokinshu* by the poet Fujiwara Teika |
| 1227 | Introduction of Soto branch of Zen from China |
| 1274 | First Mongol invasion |
| 1281 | Second Mongol invasion |

## 1333—1393 NAMBOKUCHO PERIOD
### Period of the Northern and Southern Courts

| | |
|---|---|
| 1384 | Death of Kan-ami, developer of *Noh* drama |

## 1393—1573 MUROMACHI PERIOD
### Change in the Feudal Society

| | |
|---|---|
| 1397 | Building of Kinkakuji Temple (Gold Pavilion in Kyoto) |
| 1444 | Death of Zeami, perfector of *Noh* drama |
| 1483 | Construction of Ginkakuji Temple (Silver Pavilion in Kyoto) |
| 1506 | Death of the painter monk Sesshu |
| 1549 | Arrival of St. Francis Xavier sent by the Jesuits |
| *1573* | *Establishment of **TOISHI-YA** (p. 14)* |

## 1573—1602 AZUCHI MOMOYAMA PERIOD
### Renaissance of Japanese Culture, Reestablishment of National Unity

| | |
|---|---|
| 1587 | Confiscation of the arms of the peasantry |
| 1590 | Installation of Tokugawa Ieyasu in Edo Castle as master of the *kanto* region |
| 1597 | First execution of European missionaries and Japanese converts |
| 1600 | Victory of Ieyasu at Battle of Sekigahara |

## 1600—1867 EDO PERIOD (TOKUGAWA PERIOD)

| | |
|---|---|
| 1603 | First Performance of *kabuki* by Izumo no Okuni |
| *"* | *Construction of a stone marker on Nihonbashi* |

123

124

| 1806 | Great Fire of Nihonbashi |
| *"* | *Establishment of HAIBARA* (p. 78) |
| *1813* | *Establishment of TSUMUGI-YA* (p. 106) |
| *1827* | *Completion of the Red Gate at Hongo* (p. 108) |
| *1830* | *Establishment of KYUGETSU* (p. 52) |
| *1831* | *Establishment of NAGASAWA IN-TEN* (p. 118) |
| *1833* | *Establishment of KYOSEN-DO* (p. 64) |
| *1837* | *Establishment of KUNO-YA* (p. 96) |
| 1841 | Three *kabuki* theaters moved away from Ningyo-cho |
| *1843* | *Establishment of MIYAMOTO UNOSUKE SHOTEN* (p. 12) |
| *1848* | *Establishment of KASHIWA-YA* (p. 94) |
| *1850* | *Establishment of BENMATSU* (p. 74) |
| 1853 | Arrival of Commodore Matthew C. Perry at Uraga |
| *"* | *Establishment of KANESO* (p. 10) |
| 1854 | Treaty of Kanagawa with U. S. |
| 1856 | Arrival of Consul General Townsend Harris at Shimoda |
| 1860 | Exchange in Washington of treaty ratifications by first embassy to U. S. |
| *1862* | *Establishment of FUNASA* (p. 46) |
| *"* | First Japanese embassy in Europe |
| 1863 | Bombardment of foreign vessels by Choshu forts at Shimonoseki |
| *"* | *Establishment of IWAI-SHOTEN* (p. 60) |
| 1864 | Bombardment of Shimonoseki by British, French, Dutch, and American ships |
| 1867 | Enthronment of Mutsuhito (Meiji); Tokugawa Keiki, the last *shogun* returns power to Imperial throne |

## 1868—1912 MEIJI PERIOD
### The Creation of a Modern State

| 1868 | Opening of Kobe and Osaka to foreign trade (Jan.) |
| *"* | Emperor's Charter Oath (April) |
| *"* | Establishment of Tokyo (Edo) as new capital (Nov.) |

| | |
|---|---|
| 1869 | Opening of telegraph line between Tokyo and Yokohama |
| 1870 | Permission for commoners to take surnames |
| 1872 | Opening of railway between Tokyo and Yokohama |
| 1873 | Adoption of Gregorian calendar in place of lunar calendar |
| *″* | *Establishment of HAMADA-SHOTEN* (p. 22) |
| *″* | *Establishment of ENOMOTO-EN* (p. 30) |
| *″* | *Establishment of ISERYU* (p. 58) |
| 1876 | Prohibition of carrying of swords by samurai |
| 1877 | Satsuma Rebellion and death of Saigo Takamori |
| *″* | Founding of Tokyo University |
| *1878* | *Establishment of BUNKOH-DO* (p. 26) |
| *″* | *Establishment of ISHIDA-BIWA-TEN* (p. 116) |
| 1882 | Opening of the Ueno Zoo |
| *″* | Founding of Bank of Japan |
| *″* | Founding of Waseda University |
| *1883* | *Establishment of KOTOBUKI-DO* (p. 62) |
| *″* | *Establishment of RYUZEN-DO* (p. 104) |
| *1890* | *Establishment of HASHIMOTO* (p. 34) |
| *″* | *Establishment of MAEZAWA-GOBAN-TEN* (p. 114) |
| *1893* | *Establishment of BACHI-EI* (p. 56) |
| 1894 | Completion of main building of Bank of Japan; operation of the first elevator in Japan |
| 1898 | Completion of waterworks in Tokyo |
| 1899 | Screening of the first domestic movie film at *Kabuki-za* theater |
| 1903 | Construction of the first street car route in Tokyo |
| 1903 | Opening of Hibiya Park |
| *1912* | *Establishment of KYOYA* (p. 38) |

## 1912—1926 TAISHO PERIOD

The Appearance of Liberal Democratic Trends

## 1926— SHOWA PERIOD

War, Occupation and Postwar Japan

| | |
|---|---|
| *1948* | *Establishment of BINGOYA* (p. 110) |
| 1947 | New Constitution goes into effect |
| *"* | Enactment of economic deconcentration law |
| 1949 | Uniform exchange rate of 360 yen to the dollar ordered by MacArthur |
| 1950 | Invasion of South Korea by North Korea |
| 1950 | Kinkakuji Temple (Gold Pavilion in Kyoto) burnt down |
| 1951 | Signing of peace treaty with 48 nations and security pact with U. S. at San Francisco |

* * *

# GLOSSARY AND INDEX

## A

**age:** thinly-sliced and deep-fried *tofu* 68

**agemono:** 80

**age-no-dekitate:** fried *tofu* hot out of the pan 68

**Amida:** Buddha Amida; the Lord of Infinite Light; the most widely worshipped of all the Buddhas 22

**anago:** sea eel 46

**asari:** a kind of clam 46

**ashida:** *geta* for rainy days 32

## B

**bachi:** a plectrum 56

**baika:** one of the *mukusa no takimono* (six secret Imperial incenses) used in early spring; literally, "plum blossom" 98

**bajo-chochin:** lanterns carried while on horseback 94

**bancha:** the cheapest kind of green tea made from larger, tougher leaves 30

**bandai-tsumugi:** 106

**bangasa:** umbrellas made of golden-brown oiled paper; less expensive than *janome* 32

**Banshu soroban:** abacuses produced in Hyogo Prefecture which was called Banshu before the Meiji Period 16

**bento:** picnic lunch 74

**bijin-ga:** a category of *ukiyo-e*, portraits of beautiful women 40

**bincho:** expensive charcoal of high heating power, produced in Wakayama Prefecture 8

**biwa:** Japanese lute 116

**bon-odori:** a folk dance performed at *Bon*, the season of the festival for the dead, which lasts from August (or July) 13 to 15 54

**bonsai-basami:** miniature tree clippers 70

**Boy's Day:** a festival held on May 5 when people decorate their homes with armor and helmets and fly gigantic paper carp from tall poles outside their doors. The festival's name has been officially changed to

Children's Day, but it is still popularly called Boys' Day. The decorations symbolize masculine strength and the ability to overcome difficulties. 52

**bunraku:** traditional Japanese puppet theater

**butsudan:** Buddhist altars 22

**butsugu:** general name for Buddhist altars and decorations 22

## C

**cha-dogu:** utensils used in the tea ceremony 104

**chiyogami:** Japanese craft paper which is colored or tie-dyed in traditional designs; used for making doll's cloths or miniature decorations 78

**chochin:** paper lanterns 94

**chuban:** 40

**chu-zao:** a kind of *shamisen* with a medium-thick neck. 56

## D

**daimyo:** feudal lord of a province 54

**Date:** family name of the lord who reigned in the Sendai Province during the Edo Period 86

**dobin:** teapot with a half-circle detachable handle usually made of bamboo 58

**Dogu-ya:** a classic *rakugo* story about various kinds of tool-dealers 70

**dorayaki:** pancake filled with dark bean jam 42

## E

**ebi:** shrimp 46

**Echigo-jofu:** linen crepe bleached in the ultra-violet rays of the sun which are reflected against deep snow; a unique product of Niigata Prefecture 106

**Edo:** early name for Tokyo 18

**Edokko:** a 3rd-generation resident of Tokyo, usually from the Kanda area; he is typically hot tempered, gay and generous. 88

**Edo no tebineri:** 20

**Edo Period:** name of the historical period from 1615 to 1868; also called Tokugawa Period 20, 40

**Edo-shumi-kogangu:** elaborate hand-made miniatures of Edo-Period life 20

**Emperor Seiwa:** an emperor who reigned in the middle of 9th century and whose descendants became the Minamoto, the head family of the great medieval warrior clan called the Genji 52

**F**

**fude:** writing or painting brush 50

**fude-kake:** a small bamboo rack for writing brushes 50

**fukuromono:** a traditional style of handbag to be worn with a kimono 96

**fukuro-obi:** women's sash made of silk with the design in several places 76

**fumibako:** letter box 38

**funayado:** an establishment that rents boats 48

**furo-oke:** a traditional deep wooden bathtub favored by Japanese because of its ability to hold the heat and its refreshing scent 92

**fusuma:** sliding paper door 78

**futatsu-giri:** 40

**fuzoku:** a category of *ukiyo-e*; scenery or the life of the city 40

**G**

**gagaku:** ancient Court music which accompanies *bugaku* dances performed in the Imperial Palace and some of the more celebrated Shinto shrines 12

**gampi:** soft, smooth, semi-transparent hand-made paper good for calligraphy 78

**gammodoki:** a fried patty of *tofu* with bits of mixed vegetables 68

**Genji Clan:** a powerful association of warrior clans centered around the Minamoto family in the Kanto area in eastern Japan 52

**gemmaicha:** *bancha* (green tea) mixed with roasted and popped rice 30

**geta:** wooden clogs, which are still popularly worn today and produce a lovely sound when they go click click on the pavement 32

**Girls' Day Festival:** a festival for girls, held on March 3, with elaborate miniature dolls representing the ancient Emperor and Empress and their court 64

**go:** a game played on a special board with 180 white stones and 181 black stones. The object of the game is to obtain more space than the opponent 114

**goban:** *go* board with 19 horizontal and 19 vertical lines on whose intersections players alternately lay stones 114

**gobo:** the long white root of the burdock 46

**gofuku:** the general name for Japanese clothes 100

**goishi:** *go* stones 114

**gusoku:** a suit of armor 84

**gyokuro:** the best and most expensive grade of green tea 30

**H**

**haiku:** Japanese verse-form of 17 syllables arranged in pattern of 5-7-5 78

**haiko-ningyo:** a crawling baby doll with movable head, arms and legs 52

**hai-otoshi:** tobacco box with drawers and copper-lined ashtray 38

**Hakata-obi:** men's and women's sash, usually striped, so called because it was originally made at Hakata in Kyushu 76

**hampen:** soft fish-paste cake 80

**han:** a family seal, used in place of signature 118

**hanao:** the thongs of the *geta* 32

**hana-basami:** flower clippers 70

**hana-oke:** a wooden flower basket 92

**hangetsu:** 80

**hanko:** a family seal, used in place of signature 118

**haori:** jacket worn over a kimono 100

**haori-jime:** short cords that fasten the kimono jacket 26

**haribako:** sewing box with elevated pin cushion and drawers 38

**hasami:** scissors 70

**han-namagashi:** general name for tiny elaborate, half-soft tea cakes and candies which stay fresh for a long time 70

**haze:** goby; a fish especially good for tempura 46

**higashi:** general name for dry, tiny elaborate tea cakes or candies which stay fresh for a long time　70

**hina-ningyo:**　dolls for the Girls' Day Festival　52

**hito-kuchi-anago:**　48

**hocho:**　cutlery　10

**honyaki:**　a technique of tempering iron to make Japanese swords and cutlery　10

**hojicha:**　roasted *bancha* (green tea) leaves　30

**hoki:**　broom　82

**hoso:**　102

**hoso-zao:**　a kind of *shamisen* with a thin neck　56

**hugu hiki:**　a professional knife with a slender blade used at Japanese restaurants to cut blowfish　10

**Hyakunin-isshu:**　card game played by 3 or more players with two sets of a hundred ancient 31-syllable poem cards.　58

**hyottoko:**　a round-eyed male figure with an off-center mouth who often appears in Shinto religious dances at festivals　12

**I**

**ichi-mai:**　8

**igusa:**　rush, a plant grown on marshy land　112

**Ikutaryu:**　a school of koto playing using finger picks with flat ends　86

**Intangible Cultural Property and Living National Treasure:**　titles established under the Cultural Properties Protection Law of 1950. The Law protects and preserves not only art objects like paintings and antique vases, but also the intangible skills needed to produce those objects. (The Law also applies to the techniques of the performing arts.) When a skill, such as a particular kind of fabric dyeing, is designated an Intangible Cultural Property, the honor goes to a craftsman who has mastered that skill. The craftsman becomes known as a Living National Treasure　28

**ishogi:**　a type of doll for the Girls' Day Festival; dolls wearing a realistic, traditional kimono usually made of silk　52

**it-cho:**　68

**itojime-daiko:** hourglass-shaped drums which have horsehide coverings strung together with a silk cord 12

## J

**janome:** umbrellas with brightly colored oiled paper or silk; more expensive than *bangasa* 32

**jibori:** 12

**jijyu:** one of the Emperor's six secret incenses; literally, "Imperial Chamberlain" 98

**jinrikisha or ricksha:** 2-wheeled carriage pulled by 1 or 2 men 44

**jo-nama-gashi:** elaborate and expensive tea cakes 42

## K

**kabuki:** a type of ancient drama, based on singing and dancing, with many spectacular scenes. Created in the 17th century and enjoyed by the common people, it exerted great influence over bourgeois culture 18

**kagura:** an old form of humorous entertainment performed at shrines on certain festival days 12

**kaku-obi:** men's narrow and dark-colored sash 76

**kama:** a wooden tool which measures the curve of each section of a wooden bucket 92

**kamaboko:** fish cake 74

**Kamakura Period:** the historical period (1199-1333) 112

**kana-fude:** brushes for writing *kana* syllabaries 50

**kanji-fude:** brushes for writing Chinese calligraphy 50

**Kan-non:** Japanese name for Kuan Yin, goddess of Mercy 22

**Kansai:** name of the region composed of Kyoto, Osaka, Nara, Kobe and environs 10

**Kanto:** name of the region composed of Tokyo and the surrounding prefectures of Kanagawa, Saitama, Gumma, Tochigi, Ibaraki and Chiba 38

**kashi-yoji:** a long toothpick used for cutting and eating cakes 66

**katana:** Japanese sword 84

**katate:** small wooden scoops used to pour water over the body before stepping into a Japanese bath 92

**Kotai Jingu:** Ise Grand Shrine; the headquarters of Japanese Shintoism  22

**koten-tsumugi:**  106

**koto:** Japanese harp  86

**kotoh:** antique swords made from the 9th to the 17th century  84

**kuchi-nashi:** gardenia; also means "without a mouth"  114

**kujaku-fude:** peacock-feather brushes  50

**Kuniyoshi:** prolific printmaker of the *ukiyo-e* school (1797–1861)  66

**kurenai-kai:** an association of geisha at Ningyo-cho  54

**kurobou:** one of the six secret Imperial incenses used all year round  98

**kuromoji:** camphor-tree  66

**kuroyaki:** anything charred  36

**kusa-mochi:** a spring tea cake: a green rice cake flavored with a delicious and fragrant kind of grass  42

**kushi:** comb  18

**Kutani:** name of a district in Ishikawa Prefecture, famous for porcelain. Old Kutani is known for its remarkable design while new Kutani is better known for its green and golden color  58

**kuwa:** mulberry  38

**kyo-hana oridashi:**  78

**kyusu:** teapot with a projecting handle made from the same material as the pot  58

## L

**Living National Treasure:** a title of a man who is designated for his very outstanding skill or ability in preserving traditional Japanese arts, music and drama. See Intangible Cultural Property.  100

## M

**magemono:** a round, shallow wooden box containing a gift assortment of *tsukudani* (fish tidbits), or tiny colorful Japanese candies  46

**maru-obi:** women's sash made of silk brocade with the design running the entire length; usually the most expensive 76

**matsuge-nuki:** tweezers for removing inverted eyelashes 70

**Meiji Restoration:** a coup d'état carried out in 1868 against the Tokugawa rule by Satsuma (Kagoshima Pref.), Chōshu (Yamaguchi Pref.), Tosa (Kōchi Pref.) and some other domains to restore the Imperial rule 70, 84, 98

**Meiji Shrine:** a famous Shinto shrine in Tokyo, dedicated to Emperor Meiji who was responsible for opening the doors of Japan to the world 12

**meishi:** calling card 118

**menuki:** small metal ornaments on sword handles 84

**Michio Miyagi:** a *koto* master who developed and composed new *koto* music called *shin nihon ongaku* 86

**mikoshi:** portable festival shrine 12

**mingei:** folkcraft 110

**mingeihin:** articles of folkcraft 110

**misu:** bamboo shade, with silk binding and elaborate tassels, often hung along the corridor of a shrine or temple 82

**Miyairi Shohei:** well known swordsmith; a Living National Treasure 14

**mizu-fude:** a kind of brush made by a complicated and difficult technique developed in the 11th century 50

**mizutaki:** chicken, vegetables and *tofu* cooked at the table 68

**momen-dofu:** the basic kind of *tofu* having a rough texture 68

**momo:** peach 42

**Mukusa no takimono:** the six secret incenses of the Imperial Family 98

**Musume-dojoji:** a popular Japanese dance in which a player appears with a wistaria spray on her shoulder 52

**ochazuke:** a bowl of rice over which has been poured a fish or tea broth, to be eaten with *tsukudani*, or pickles 46

**ochiba:** one of the six secret Imperial incenses used in early winter; literally, "fallen leaves" 98

**oden:** a mixture of fish paste cakes, tofu cubes, vegetables boiled in a large pot of fish bouillon; good with *sake* and often sold outside on the streets at night by wagon vendors 94

**oden-dane:** ingredients of *oden* 80

**odori-obi:** traditional Japanese dancer's sash 76

**"O-Edo Nihonbashi":** a song describing *daimyos* passing over the Nihonbashi bridge 72

**ohban:** 40

**ohdaiko:** large, barrel-shaped drums with cowhide tacked to each end 12

**ohgi:** fans 64

**o-himo:** decorative silk cords used for many purposes 28

**o-hitsu:** wooden container to keep cooked rice warm 92

**okame:** funny, fat-cheeked female figure which often appears in Shinto religious dances at festivals 12

**oke:** wooden tubs and buckets 92

**Onna-keizu:** a classic Meiji novel written by Izumi Kyoka who was a leader of romanticism and influenced Tanizaki Junichiro. His novels often appear in *shimpa* plays 46

**onigara-yaki:** charcoal-broiled seasoned shrimp heads 48

**orizume:** box lunch 74

**O-seibo:** a year-end gift 8

**R**

**rakugo:** comic stories full of puns, told by a professional storyteller 70

**reiku-zen:** tiny offering dishes for serving food for the dead on *Bon* Festival 22

**Rokka-sen:** 30

**Ryōgoku kawabiraki:** River-opening festival of fireworks, held in the middle of July near the Ryogoku-bashi on the Sumida River 6

# S

**sageo:** decorative cords for swords 28

**sakura-mochi:** a spring tea cake; a delicate pink sweet wrapped in a pickled cherry leaf 42

**samurai:** a feudal warrior 14

**Sano Ichimatsu:** 52

**saru:** monkey 66

**sashi-gushi:** decorative comb 18

**sashimi bōcho:** a slender, long knife used by both housewives and professionals to slice fresh raw fish 10

**sashimono:** cabinetwork 38

**Satsuma-biwa:** a type of *biwa* on which heroic, inspirational songs are played 116

**sembei:** cracker made from rice-flour dough, often seasoned with soy sauce 8

**Sencha:** a form of tea ceremony in which the most expensive tea called *gyokuro* is served and tasted 104

**sencha:** the most common tea, medium priced and usually served to guests 30

**sendai-dansu:** thinly lacquered *tansu* decorated with round iron plates made of "nanbu-tetsu," a famous ironware produced close to Sendai City 38

**Senke Family:** descendants of Sen no Rikyu 104

**senkoh:** a stick of incense used exclusively in Buddhist Memorial rituals for the dead 98

**Sen no Rikyo:** the famous tea master, connoisseur and arbiter of taste who taught his followers to appreciate the beauty and simplicity of every-day Korean pottery 104

**sensu:** fans 64

**seto-mono:** porcelain, pottery 58

**shamisen:** a musical instrument with three strings on a long thin neck and a square sound box, which the player strikes with a large plectrum held in his right hand 56

**sha-in:** a company's name seal 118

**shigure:** shellfish *tsukudani* which originated at Kuwana in Mie Prefecture 46

**shikishi:** square-shaped card-paintings 26

**shimpa:** a new drama form of the Meiji Period which combined Western and *Kabuki* elements 18

**Shibai-machi:** name of a district close to Ningyo-cho which was a center for theatrical entertainments in the Edo Period 54

**shinkokugeki:** a new type of popular drama with battle scenes and melodramatic stories. Founded by Shojiro Sawada in 1917, the first successful performance was held in the Meiji-za theater at Ningyo-cho 54

**shin-mingei:** articles of folkcraft still being produced and used today 110

**shin nihon ongaku:** a new Japanese music which developed in the 1920's in which Japanese musical instruments are used to play Western music 86

**shin-shintoh:** antique swords made from 1830 to the Meiji Restoration 84

**Shinto:** the national religion of Japan; the worship of the Sun Goddess and other deities based on a broad worship of the wonders and mysteries of nature with a sense of awe 22

**shintoh:** antique swords made from 17th century to 1830 84

**shirasu:** tiny white fish 46

**shogi:** Japanese chess 114

**Shogun:** title of the military dictators of Japan prior to the Meiji Era 54

**shuniku:** red ink pad used for *hanko* (name seals) 118

**soroban:** Japanese abacus 16

**St. Luke's Hospital:** one of the best hospitals in Tokyo established at the beginning of the Meiji Period when many foreigners settled close to the site of the hospital 90

**sudare:** bamboo or reed shade for decoration or room separation 82

**Suehiro Tei:** a well-known *rakugo* theater 70

**sukiyaki:** thin slices of high quality beef, various vegetables and *tofu* cooked lightly in a sauce of sake, sugar and soy sauce and eaten dipped in raw egg 68

**sumo:** Japanese wrestling; fought between two wrestlers who try to push the opponent out of the ring, or force him to touch the sand of the ring with any part of his body  44

**sushi:** cooked rice flavored with vinegar, salt and sugar, and used in three forms: small oval mounds covered with raw or cooked fish, mixed with cooked vegetables and eggs, or rolled in sheets of *nori* seaweed  92

**sushi-oke:** a shallow wooden tub in which vinegared rice for sushi is mixed  92

**suzume-yaki:** an hors d'oeuvre of tiny crucian carp grilled over charcoal and seasoned with sweet soy sauce  48

**Sword Abolition Law:** a law passed at the beginning of the Meiji Period which forbade the *samurai* and common people to keep and carry swords  28

# T

**tabi:** traditional Japanese socks worn with *zori* or *geta*  102

**tachi-basami:** Western scissors  70

**taiko:** drums  12

**tako:** brightly colored paper kites used by children at New Year's time  34

**tansu:** a chest of drawers made in several stackable sections  38

**tanzaku:** rectangular-shaped card-paintings  26

**tatami:** floor mats consisting of 2 inches of solid straw padding covered with a rush matting  110, 112

**tatemono:** the name for hanging scrolls with long centers  26

**tawara-gashi**  70

**tebunko:** letter-boxes  60

**tekagami:** albums containing the calligraphy of famous historical persons  26

**tenugui:** small brightly-patterned cotton cloths used as scarves in Japanese dances and festivals, or tied around the head. Also, a term for small bath towels  102

**tofu:** soybean curd  68, 74

# W

**wa-gashi:** general name for Japanese cakes   62

**waka:** Japanese verse form of 31 syllables arranged in a pattern of 5-7-5 7-7   78

**wari-in:** revenue stamp   118

**washi:** Japanese hand-made paper   78

**waso komono:** kimono accessories   96

# Y

**Yakichi Yoshida:** a scissors craftman, the first to make Western-styles cissors in Japan   70

**yaki-dofu:** *tofu* broiled on top for firmness and flavor, used in *nabemono*, *sukiyaki* or *mizutaki*   68

**yakkodako:** a kite shaped like a man or bird; very easy for children to fly because it has wings   32

**yakusha-e:** a category of *ukiyo-e*; portraits of *kabuki* actors   40

**yanagi:**   102

**yakata-bune:** roofed pleasure boat   48

**yaku-shoku-in:** a company executive's seal   118

**Yamadaryu:** a school of *koto* playing using picks with a rounded end   86

**yoji:** toothpicks   66

**yojoto:**   70

**yokomono:** the name for hanging scrolls with wide centers   26

**yoroi:** armor   84

**yukata:** a brightly patterned cotton kimono for summer wear   100

**yuki-geta:** *geta* for snowy days   32

**Yuki-tsumugi:** a finely woven silk fabric from the district around Yuki City, produced with incredibly painstaking efforts; one of the most expensive kimono materials   106

**yumihari-chochin:** a cylindrical lantern with a handle and hook for hanging on the wall   94

# Z

**zansa-bukuro:** an elegant folding box for taking home leftovers from a tea ceremony or restaurant meal